Elizabeth F. Schwartz has been practicing law since 1997 and is one of the nation's best-known advocates for the legal rights of the lesbian, gay, bisexual, and transgender community. Her law practice focuses on family formation (adoption, insemination, and surrogacy), divorce, estate planning, and probate. Schwartz lives in Miami.

elizabethschwartz.com
@SchwartzOutLaw

Jim Obergefell has held a variety of corporate jobs in training and technology. He is the named plaintiff in *Obergefell v. Hodges* and is the co-author of *Love Wins*. *Politico* named him one of the fifty top visionaries of 2015. He lives in Washington, D.C.

BEFORE I DO

BEFORE I DO

A LEGAL GUIDE TO MARRIAGE, GAY AND OTHERWISE

ELIZABETH F. SCHWARTZ

THE NEW PRESS

NEW YORK
LONDON

Requests for permission to reproduce selections from this book should be mailed to: Permissions
Department, The New Press, 120 Wall Street, 31st floor, New York, NY 10005.

Published in the United States by The New Press, New York, 2016
Distributed by Perseus Distribution

ISBN 9781620971550 (e-book)

LIBRARY OF CONGRESS CATALOGING-IN-PUBLICATION DATA

Names: Schwartz, Elizabeth F.
Title: Before I do : a legal guide to marriage, gay and otherwise / Elizabeth
    F. Schwartz.
Description: New York ; London : New Press, [2016] | Includes index.
Identifiers: LCCN 2016014074 | ISBN 9781620971543 (pb)
Subjects: LCSH: Same-sex marriage—Law and legislation—United
    States—Popular works. | Same-sex marriage—United States—Psychological
    aspects—Popular works. | Gays—Legal status, laws, etc.—United
    States—Popular works. | Gays—United States—Finance, Personal—Popular
    works.
Classification: LCC KF539 .S39 2016 | DDC 346.7301/68—dc23 LC record available at
http://lccn.loc.gov/2016014074

The New Press publishes books that promote and enrich public discussion and understanding of
the issues vital to our democracy and to a more equitable world. These books are made possible
by the enthusiasm of our readers; the support of a committed group of donors, large and small;
the collaboration of our many partners in the independent media and the not-for-profit sector;
booksellers, who often hand-sell New Press books; librarians; and above all by our authors.

www.thenewpress.com

Photograph of Elizabeth F. Schwartz by Alexis Rodriguez-Duarte in collaboration with Tico Torres

Book design and composition by Bookbright Media
This book was set in Bembo and News Gothic Std

Printed in the United States of America

10 9 8 7 6 5 4 3 2 1

For my father, of cherished memory

And to Lyd, best of wives and best of women

CONTENTS

BEFORE I DO

1
FROM OUTLAWS TO IN-LAWS

You don't really need to get married, but marriage is
awfully nice.

—*Lily Tomlin*

After a long battle, the Supreme Court of the United States determined that same-sex relationships are legitimate and worthy
of recognition, both at the federal level and in all fifty states. The
Obergefell case, decided in June 2015, brought uniformity to a hodge-
podge of rights and responsibilities that varied from state to state for
same-sex couples. Now we lesbian, gay, bisexual, and transgender
(LGBT) people are free to commit to each other under the law of
every state, and our commitments must be recognized nationwide.

Not long ago, same-sex couples had to jump through endless
hoops to make our relationships akin to a legally recognized marriage. Often we had to work around the law, play the system, and
find the loopholes. Denied the right to be at the hospital bedside of
our sick partners, some claimed to be siblings and therefore next
of kin. When we could not adopt as an openly gay couple, we hid
our relationships and adopted children as individuals, not reveal-
ing our true families. In some cases we adopted *one another*, creating a fictional but legal parent-child relationship, just to acquire
rights that the law refused to confer on same-sex couples. Creating
contracts and using inventive estate planning tools, equality-focused
lawyers legitimized our relationships as much as possible. Lawyers

accustomed to operating within the confines of the law figured out how to work on the fringes in order to achieve basic protections for gay and lesbian couples within the law.

For the most part, those days are over. We no longer have to operate as outlaws—and we can have in-laws! But here's the rub: many LGBT couples, accustomed to living off the grid and in the margins, are so thrilled to have the opportunity to marry that we are gleefully jumping into marriage headfirst, without concern for the legal and financial consequences. It is easy to get caught up in the excitement over the victories we have achieved, especially when there is a societal expectation that each and every loving and committed couple ought to marry, an act often considered one of life's milestones. Before racing to the altar, it is important to understand that the law can be treacherous. If you are considering marriage, remember this: just because you *can* get married does not mean you *should*.

For twenty years I have been helping LGBT families create and dissolve relationships in a particularly hostile legal environment— the wacky, backward state of Florida. I have counseled thousands of individuals and couples who failed to plan properly as they formed unions and families. Failing to plan has terrible consequences. Holding the hands of devastated clients, I only wish that they had consulted me earlier. That is why I wrote this book.

Before I Do is for couples who have been coloring outside the lines and now are considering making their relationship legal. It explains what marriage means—and does not mean. It spells out all the implications of marriage in a straightforward, easy-to-follow style.

Now that we can freely say "I do," we need to know the answers to a few simple questions:

- What are the income tax consequences of marrying?
- If you split, what happens to your kids, your assets, and your property?
- If you pass away, what happens to your kids, your assets, and your property?
- Does your spouse or potential spouse have debt? Can a creditor come after you for your spouse's debts? What can you do about it?

- What if you have children from a prior relationship? How can you protect them?
- Will you co-parent children? What legal relationship will you have with the children? Are you committing through your actions to child support?
- What if you inherit during your marriage? Is that inheritance shared between you?

If you care enough to enter into the very solemn act of marriage, treat it with the respect it deserves, and exercise caution. Too many couples jump into marriage without a full sense of the consequences or acknowledgment that a legal marriage is a contract entered into with your state to be governed by the laws and regulations concerning domestic relations, even if some of those laws did not exist at the time of the marriage! One consequence of not fully thinking through the consequences of marriage is shown in the story of Brittney Griner. As you may know if you stood on line at the supermarket near the tabloid rack, Griner is a star basketball player in the WNBA. Her amazing athletic career has been sullied by the circumstances of her brief marriage to another WNBA basketball player, Glory Johnson. Domestic violence charges preceded the marriage, and resulted in both being suspended from play for a record seven games. Just as many different-sex couples have, despite the warning signs, Griner and Johnson married in May 2015. A month later, Johnson announced that she was pregnant. The following day, Griner filed for an annulment; Johnson has requested $20,000 per month child support for the unborn child. It is unclear how the Griner-Johnson union will be dissolved, or whether Griner will be deemed a parent, but it is clear that marriage is not something to enter impulsively or without a full appreciation of the stakes involved and the consequences if the relationship does not work out. This caution applies to all couples, whether same-sex or not.

Everything always seems rosy when a couple is headed to the altar. People cannot imagine anything bad happening, especially divorce. But all couples considering marriage, gay and straight, need to consider what happens if the relationship ends. Even if you are already married, educate yourself about its consequences. It is never too late for loving couples to have a conversation about their future, nor is it ever too late to consult an attorney about how the marriage would be treated at death or divorce.

Misinformation can be even more dangerous than no information. Recently I consulted with a lovely guy; let's call him Troy. Troy married Charles, his partner of ten years. Troy assumed that after a decade together nothing could ever go wrong between them; they entered legal matrimony without the advice of a family lawyer. Troy is several years older than Charles and closer to retirement. Troy's friends—including his sister, a real estate lawyer, and a buddy who is a criminal defense attorney—all told him that he did not have to worry about his individual retirement account (IRA) because he started it before the marriage: his friends said it would remain Troy's property, no matter what. Troy and his friends assumed that the IRA would always be a nonmarital asset. While Troy could name Charles as a beneficiary at death, they assured him that all of the funds would remain Troy's separate property in the event of divorce. As he inched closer to retirement age, Troy began maxing out his IRA contributions, well aware that if he died, Charles could roll that IRA into his own retirement account. In case of Troy's death, Charles could also stretch out the payments if he did not need all the money, so that those funds would not put him into a higher tax bracket. Troy never imagined an end to their relationship that was not his own death. Then, seven years into the marriage, the relationship began to unravel. Charles filed for divorce. Charles's savvy lawyer asserted Charles's right to the appreciation in value of the retirement account over the term of the marriage, as the contributions made from Troy's income are considered marital income—even if the IRA was in Troy's name alone. The increase in the IRA due to marital contributions and the market appreciation on those contributions over their seven-year marriage was $90,000. Troy was shocked when I told him that indeed, according to the laws of the state of Florida, he needed to pay $45,000 to his soon-to-be-ex. He wished that he had sought accurate advice before he tied the knot. I wish he had too. I could have helped to protect him from this costly mistake or he could have knowingly made the decision to have his spouse share in the marital portion of the account, even if their relationship was terminated by divorce.

Before I Do is for all married people and for those thinking about formalizing a union. Many same-sex couples have obtained real estate and mortgages together, commingled bank accounts, and established joint credit cards. Some people who suffered in previous relationships believe they learned the hard way how to protect themselves and their assets. Others believe they are doing a good job in their household accounting. Everyone needs to understand that legal marriage adds new rights and responsibilities. What rights and obligations does marriage confer and what rights and obligations does it not provide? This book will help you to answer that question.

For younger gay and lesbian people who are beginning to accumulate assets and just starting their first serious relationship, *Before I Do* shines a light on the basic issues of marriage and outlines the steps necessary to ensure both parties are protected to the full extent of the law.

The consequences of marriage are the same for everyone. *All* couples considering marriage, gay or straight, should be deliberate. For gay and lesbian people, marriage is a new social and legal benefit; it has not been a part of our community's consciousness or history. We have only had the freedom to marry for a short time. Until now gays and lesbians have largely not entered into relationships with an eye toward "until death do us part," not because we are unwilling or unable to commit but largely because the law has not recognized the potential of our relationships. It was difficult to treat our relationships seriously when the laws of our nation did not. Many of us knew we were gay, lesbian, bisexual, or transgender from a young age and therefore never imagined we would ever enter into a marriage as traditional as those we saw in our families or in popular culture. Some of us objected to marriage from a feminist perspective; others simply never conceived of marriage as a realistic option because of the unconventional ways in which they structured relationships. A good proportion of LGBT people unequivocally said they never thought they would live to see marriage as an option for us anywhere, much less throughout the United States.

The ins and outs of marriage are foreign to many of us. As a community, we are not prepared by generations of conversation about how to make our relationships last with others of the same gender. We cannot be expected to know automatically what happens if marriage does not work. LGBT people have not lived in a world with premarital guidance for LGBT couples. We have suffered systematic exclusion from many of our communities of faith, a space where traditionally some version of marital preparation happens. We have not been a part of locker room conversations that include cautions about prenuptial agreements and the distribution of marital assets. Once the freedom to marry became law, many same-sex couples faced the supposition that we would marry pronto; if we did not, we faced questions about our commitment. Many assumed that the sole reason we were not married was because legally we could not be; once the law changed, these same people thought that certainly we all would race to the altar.

Pent-up demand for equality leads some to act impetuously. We all know at least one couple, swept up in the moment at a gay pride event, who got hitched. Through my law practice, my public speaking, and colleagues who practice LGBT family law around the country, I have become aware of quite a number of such couples. News flash: those festive cocktail-soaked nuptials are real marriages, too, folks, with all of the consequences of marriage. (Check out Debra Guston's pitch-perfect "Why I Got Married" in Chapter 8.)

Others have wisely taken a different, more deliberate approach, and some choose not to approach the altar at all. For couples not on the same page about marriage, the exciting developments from the U.S. Supreme Court have been a source of tension in their relationships.

For some couples, marriage imbued their relationships with seriousness and stability. Many couples report that after marrying they feel safe enough to take new risks—quitting a job to take care of children, starting a new entrepreneurial venture, or taking some other life risk.

While I hope lots of straight couples will read this book—the information in it broadly applies to any two people considering marriage—the relative novelty of marriage for same-sex couples makes us the primary focus. All couples need to understand not only what *getting* married means, but also what *being* married means. The initial glow of romance, the excitement of planning a wedding and being a bride or groom, can blind us to the long-term implications of a marriage, even a successful one. I am not trying to discourage anyone from legally formalizing commitments. I fought long and hard with thousands of other advocates for our freedom to marry. Social science research suggests that marriage has positive effects on our physical and mental health, especially as we age. A strong marriage can be the cornerstone of a healthy, successful family. I am part of a blended family, a Brady Bunch of my own that includes biological and adopted children. When my parents married, each of them brought children from prior marriages. My father had three biological children and adopted the two little boys who had been adopted by my mother and her ex-husband. Then, together, they had me, the youngest of six. They remained very happily married for more than forty-five years, until my beloved father passed away. We had our share of the usual blended-family problems, but I watched how the bond of my parents' marriage kept my creatively assembled family united and thriving.

I am grateful that my partner and I were able to affirm our commitment through legal marriage. After eleven years together, we knew we were in it to win it. After talking to our accountant and getting her blessing (so romantic!), my partner and I reviewed the various benefits that would be available to us only if we were married, and we balanced those against the potential risks. During our deliberations, my father and my soon-to-be spouse's mother were suffering prolonged illnesses. We wanted them to know while they were alive that we were married, especially given that they both particularly prized marriage as a signifier of stability and safety. We married in Vermont in 2013, three weeks after the *Windsor* decision, the U.S. Supreme Court case that repealed the core of the Defense of Marriage Act (DOMA) and made meaningful federal benefits available even for couples living in nonrecognition states (which included Florida until January 2015).

What was most interesting to us was not that we felt different as a married couple—we did—but that marriage brought a sense of commitment and permanence to our lives. A friend well described his marriage to his partner of fifteen years as feeling like "a back door had closed." It was also fascinating to note how other people regarded us differently. One of my nephews, who has known my wife and me for roughly the same amount of time, said upon our marriage that he now has another "aunt." Funny, I thought she was his aunt anyway. To him, the government sanctioning of our relationship made it official now. One of my brothers, who is the closest to my wife and the most supportive of our relationship since day one, said upon our marriage that now she had a "vote" in the family. Of course, for many years when something of any import was percolating, my mother would call our home and ask for my partner to be put on the phone rather than me because it seems that the two of them instinctively have the same point of view. I think my partner had long had a vote in the family. Still, for my straight family members, our relationship was now in a category they could understand. They speak a language whose definitional boundaries I never quite appreciated until I was initiated as a member of the exclusive marital club.

My partner and I resisted the traditional aspects of matrimony. We were ambivalent about the whole concept of marriage itself. It was not anything that either of us imagined as little girls. My other half, who came out at age six, never *ever* thought she would be able to marry and so never harbored any wedding-day bridal fantasies. We both felt just a little like we were "selling out" our community of legal outsiders by joining something so very traditional. I was ambivalent about marrying outside of my home state of Florida while I was still waging the legal battle within Florida for the right to marry. It took us a while to be comfortable using the word "wife." To us, more than the word "husband," "wife" seems loaded. It conjured decidedly antifeminist notions of ironing clothes and cooking dinner not for oneself but for the other. "Wife" almost always comes with the pronoun "my" before it and the possessive connotations that arise from centuries of coverture, the system by which a wife's identity and property were subsumed by her husband, stripping her of all independence. Slowly, though, we have come to the conclusion that there is something deliciously subversive about using that title, especially as people scratch their heads for a moment when they hear a woman referring to her wife. I remember my well-meaning father asking us after our marriage, "Which one is the wife?" "We both are, Daddy," I answered.

Embracing the term "wife" solves the problem of what to call one another. "Girlfriend" has been co-opted by straight women to refer to their female friends; "lover" is too graphic and makes me want to pronounce it with a slightly raised eyebrow and French accent; "partner" is confusing for a lawyer or anyone in business; "significant other" hardly rolls off the tongue; and "spouse" seems a bit formal. Having a definitive word choice also helps our allies and friends who stumble over what to call us. "Spouse" and "spouses" (or, as I call them, "spice"—after all, since two mouses are "mice," two spouses must be "spice") are the terms I use throughout this book. When inquiring minds ask what term to use when a couple is married, "spouse" is the one I find myself suggesting, even though it feels rather uptight. The flip side of these word games is that many expect that all same-sex couples are in fact married *and* prefer terms that reference their connubial status. Do not assume. Language is charged; do not be afraid to ask someone what terms she or he prefers that you use.

I hope that LGBT married couples can be a catalyst for change, challenging assumptions about what marriage looks like generally. As is common among same-sex couples, there are many ways in which I fulfill—and many ways that I challenge—the traditional role of "wife"; the same is true for my beloved. Similarly, there are characteristics and roles each of us inhabits historically thought of as those of a "husband." We both embody and defy all of the traditional roles. Our way works for us.

With the right information, and coming from a very different cultural perspective, LGBT people collectively can transform the imperfect institution of marriage. Maybe gay and lesbian couples will enter into marriage more mindfully and continue to arrange our relationships in a more egalitarian way. Certainly we are already changing what connotations words carry with them. As more LGBT couples marry, have children, and divide family obligations equitably without regard for the traditional gender roles, it may well become the norm for both parents to take family leave when having a child and to share parenting and family care obligations. Marriage equality is part of a broader cultural shift. We are only beginning to imagine how all of our lives might change.

Some specific notes about using this book: I sometimes say things more than once because I expect you might not read this book in a linear way. You might jump around and read only the sections that seem relevant. You might buy this book at one stage of your relationship and then put it on the bookshelf to be picked up at yet another. I try to cross-reference the other times that the information is given; the index can be a great help in navigating the book for specific information.

I am not saying anything terribly new in this book: for adroit researchers, most of this information is available somehow, somewhere. My experience, however, is that folks do not do exhaustive research before getting hitched or rely upon the misinformation provided through movies or anecdotal information from friends. *Before I Do* compiles and summarizes the research for you and provides it all in one perky package, including cameo appearances from some of the brightest professionals working with LGBT families in varied practice areas. Those cameos enrich the text with diverse perspectives and experiences, and I am grateful and proud to be able to include them.

To enliven some of the issues raised throughout the book, we use the stories of hypothetical couples to illustrate different scenarios that arise with marriage and shine a light on a few examples of the legal challenges that same-sex couples face. These and other examples throughout the book represent composites of clients and friends, with names, details, genders, and other specifics changed to protect privacy. When I refer to a particular couple from time to time, it is easy to flip back to where the couple is first introduced to be reminded of the basic narrative.

A few notes about language: I use the term "LGBT" throughout to encompass all people who identify as lesbian, gay, bisexual, transgender, intersex, questioning, and queer. I use first person ("I," "we") and second person ("you") here because "they" and "them" feel alienating. We are all one community; this book reflects that unity. Pronouns randomly shift between male and female to avoid trying to encompass all genders in each sentence. Forgive the laziness, but it reads better.

Before I Do is an educational tool. It is not a substitute for legal advice. Family and estate laws vary by state. This book highlights general issues, but I urge you to investigate further. This book is not an exhaustive review of each and every consideration and effect of marriage; it only flags the most significant issues to explore. Depending on your circumstances, you may need to see a lawyer; I hope that reading this book will make you a more informed client. To be clear (and sorry to be such a lawyer about it all), *Before I Do* does not create an attorney–client relationship between author and reader. If your situation is at all complex (and most things that look simple are not), please do see a competent, experienced professional. In the interim, this book may be the cheapest lawyer's time you will ever buy.

Having said all that, read on, learn your rights, and look before you leap!

2

A FORTY-FIVE-YEAR-LONG, PAINSTAKING BATTLE (CONDENSED TO EIGHT PAGES)

> A right is not what someone gives you; it's what no one can take from you.
>
> —*Ramsey Clark*

No book about what marriage means to gay and lesbian people would be complete without at least the most cursory review of where we have come from and how we have arrived at the freedom to marry nationwide. The freedom to marry was won by arduous door-to-door and legislator-by-legislator lobbying, by effective law-yering, and, most of all, by couples willing to share their truths and convince a nation that love is, after all, love.

There are several fantastic in-depth histories of the marriage movement. Kevin Cathcart and Leslie Gabel-Brett of Lambda Legal edited a collection called *Love Unites Us*, with contributions from lawyers, activists, and plaintiffs detailing the key legal battles beginning with *Baker v. Nelson* in 1972. In *Winning Marriage*, Marc Solomon, who was on the front lines of the marriage equality movement for years, highlights the critical victories that pushed us across the finish line; the book shines a light on the gritty work of visionaries such as Evan Wolfson, who left his position as an attorney at Lambda Legal back in 2001 to pursue his marriage work full-time at Freedom to Marry, an organization he founded, and Mary Bonauto, legal director at GLBTQ Legal Advocates and Defenders (GLAD), who represented the plaintiffs in the Massachusetts marriage case that set the ball rolling (*Goodridge v. Dept. of Public Health*, 798 N.E.2d 941 [Mass. 2003]), and who was the chief architect of the winning legal strategy for nationwide marriage equality. These books—and many others just starting to come out—tell the long history of the struggle for marriage equality. While many people think that the push for marriage equality started in the 1990s or the 2000s, gay men and lesbians were talking about marriage in the 1950s, 1960s, and 1970s. Check out movement histories such as the books mentioned above for more information.

My history in the effort for marriage equality starts with my involvement with the case in the state of Florida to secure state-wide marriage equality after the fall of DOMA through the *United States v. Windsor* case. Let me set the stage a bit regarding the fight for the freedom to marry.

In 1993, three same-sex couples in Hawaii sued to get the right to marry. The Supreme Court of Hawaii ruled in case of *Baehr v. Lewin* (74 Haw. 530, 852 P.2d 44 [1993], which later became *Baehr v. Miike*) that limiting marriage to heterosexual couples is unconstitutional discrimination. Voters then passed an amendment to the Hawaii constitution defining marriage as between a man and woman, over-turning the court decision. The Hawaii case prompted the concern that an individual state could act to grant equal access to marriage. To address this concern, the United States Congress enacted the Defense of Marriage Act (DOMA) in 1996. President Bill Clinton signed DOMA into law. DOMA was a federal law that, until struck down nearly two decades later by the U.S. Supreme Court, defined marriage as only between a man and a woman, denied the federal benefits of marriage to same-sex couples, and allowed states to refuse to recognize otherwise valid marriages of same-sex couples.

According to Section 3 of DOMA, no agency of the federal government could extend its benefits to married same-sex couples. These benefits of marriage from the federal government are substantial and varied. A report from the federal government's General Accounting Office, which undertook a sort of audit of marriage, identified 1,138 federal rights and responsibilities associated with marriage.

DOMA's Section 2 also provided that states did not need to recognize same-sex marriages performed in other states. States have long had varying rules regarding the validity of marriages, but one state refusing to honor or enforce a court order related to an otherwise valid out-of-state marriage is unconstitutional. This provision simply reinforced the barriers to marriages between people of the same gender and placated homophobes who thought allowing queer people to marry would mark the end of civilization as we know it. After DOMA's passage at the federal level, individual states began to pass their own marriage bans through legislation, constitutional amendments, and ballot initiatives until almost all states had marriage prohibitions in some form.

Marriage became the vehicle to move the LGBT rights movement forward. Activists coalesced around this goal, mindful that the right to marry affords us a dignity that makes it hard to justify discriminating against us on other grounds. Marriage is a sacred institution and a strong means through which we can get closer to the goal of full equality for our entire community. We began a full-court press, telling our stories and demanding the universal right to enter into marriage to protect ourselves and our relationships.

One of the first national wins was the overturning of DOMA by extraordinary citizen-activist Edie Windsor. Windsor and her wife, Thea Spyer, were New Yorkers who married in Canada after being together for forty-one years. Three years later, Thea passed away. Edie received bills for federal and state estate tax due on Thea's estate. The tax bill was in excess of $638,000. Edie would not owe this estate tax if their marriage had been recognized by the state of New York and the federal government, since spouses can pass an unlimited amount to each other tax-free in life and at death. Edie Windsor was not the only person in this difficult situation. Many people experienced the harms of not having their marriages recognized. With the help of the American Civil Liberties Union (ACLU), Edie sued. Her case was combined with several others to challenge the constitutionality of the ban on federal recognition of same-sex marriages in DOMA. The Supreme Court of the United States, reviewing the *Windsor* intermediate appellate court decision, agreed that DOMA violated the equal protection and due process provisions of the U.S. Constitution. In 2013 Justice Anthony Kennedy wrote in *United States v. Windsor* (570 U.S. 12):

> DOMA singles out a class of persons deemed by a State entitled to recognition and protection to enhance their own liberty. . . . DOMA instructs all federal officials, and indeed all persons with whom same-sex couples interact, including their own children, that their marriage is less worthy than the marriages of others. The federal statute is invalid, for no legitimate purpose overcomes the purpose and effect to disparage and to injure those whom the State, by its marriage laws, sought to protect in personhood and dignity. By seeking to displace this protection and treating those persons as living in marriages less respected than others, the federal statute is in violation of the Fifth Amendment. (*Windsor*, 25–26)

Roberta Kaplan, Edie Windsor's lawyer who argued her case before the Supreme Court, wrote a wonderful taxonomy of the case in her book *Then Comes Marriage: United States v. Windsor and the Defeat of DOMA*.

With this portion of DOMA struck down by the Supreme Court, marriage equality activists set about undoing the thirty-eight remaining statewide bans against marriage equality. Thus began a state-by-state march to marriage equality throughout the United States, with the powerful wind from the *Windsor* decision at our backs. We began to litigate the individual marriage bans, while LGBT activists and our many vocal allies continued those conversations about why marriage equality matters, changing hearts and minds of voters, legislators, and judges.

After *Windsor*, a group of lawyers and activists from national and statewide LGBT organizations immediately came together to decide how to take down Florida's statewide constitutional and statutory marriage bans. Within the days and weeks following *Windsor*, there were countless conference calls and email discussions to determine the quickest and most effective means to bring marriage equality to the many anxious Floridians agitating for a victory of our own. We knew that our conservative state legislature would not take action to invalidate the statutory definitions of marriage as being only between a man and a woman, and even if such a miracle happened, that would still leave in place the constitutional ban passed by voters in 2008. The constitutional ban could be repealed by a public referendum, but while polls showed that the majority of Floridians had experienced a shift in belief in the five years since the ban was passed, such a campaign would be a very costly endeavor that would take too long and require too many resources.

Folks were antsy. They were going elsewhere to wed and frustrated that they remained legal strangers back home in the Sunshine State. The decision was made to sue in Florida courts to seek a ruling that declared Florida's marriage ban an unconstitutional deprivation of the equal protection and due process rights guaranteed to all Americans. These are the same arguments that won in *Windsor* and that with each passing day were convincing more and more federal and state judges in courtrooms all over the country.

National organizations doing work on LGBT legal issues and private lawyers teamed up to bring lawsuits in courtroom after courtroom at both the federal and state levels. The victories mounted, with bans being struck down even in some of the most unlikely of states by rather conservative judges who seemed to finally understand that these bans were just pure discrimination and that same-sex marriages hurt absolutely no one and did not infringe on anyone else's rights.

Impact litigation is like filmmaking: lead players, locations, scripts, and crew are all chosen carefully. The optics of every aspect are scrutinized, including where the action is brought, what arguments are made, and who the plaintiffs are. Equality Florida, our statewide LGBT rights organization, launched a campaign called Get Engaged, to solicit stories of couples wishing to marry or to have their out-of-state marriages recognized. These couples were asked whether they would be willing to be a public face of the issue and sign on as plaintiffs in a lawsuit challenging Florida's marriage ban, and thousands of people responded. When I reviewed these submissions, I noticed that many couples wished for things that the legal institution of marriage could not give them; for example, some people wrote, "I want to get married so I can have rights to my partner's child," even though marriage does not confer that right;

see Chapter 4 for more about this. The need for a comprehensive guide to what rights marriage affords—and does *not* afford—quickly became clear to me, and was one of the inspirations for this book. Based on these submissions, a team of us selected six same-sex couples as plaintiffs, representing the gender, racial, cultural, age, and familial diversity of our community.

The National Center for Lesbian Rights brought an action in state court in Miami-Dade County. I served on the legal team, helping to craft strategy on behalf of our six plaintiff couples and the Equality Florida Institute. Judge Sarah I. Zabel heard the case, *Pareto v. Ruvin*, and issued a soaring opinion declaring the state's marriage ban unconstitutional and soon after married the first same-sex couples in Florida. There was a particular sweetness to that since Miami was the birthplace of the anti-gay bigotry that swept the nation beginning in 1977, when Anita Bryant, a former beauty queen turned professional homophobe, launched the first campaign to strip existing discrimination protections from gays and lesbians.

The ACLU of Florida and a local gay rights organization, Safeguarding American Values for Everyone (SAVE), had filed another case in federal court, and they and their amazing plaintiffs won a fantastic, sweeping victory that brought the freedom to marry and recognition for those already married to the whole state thanks to a beautiful opinion in the consolidated *Brenner* and *Grimsley* cases. Couples from across Florida were elated; at long last they could wed or have their out-of-state unions recognized.

One benefit of Florida's recognition of out-of-state same-sex marriages is that couples who wished to divorce could end their marriages without having to leave Florida (when marriages are not recognized under a particular state's law, they typically cannot be dissolved in that state). On January 6, 2015, the day the ACLU victory brought marriage equality statewide and couples were lining up to marry, I was in line at family court getting divorces for couples who had been married elsewhere and were now seeking to dissolve those unions under Florida law. Divorce lawyers realized that the right to legal love would also mean an uptick in family court dockets when same-sex couples sought to divorce, and they started to salivate over this new crop of cases.

While state after state followed the *Windsor* constitutional analysis, we suffered a few losses. The losses resulted in additional appeals to the United States Supreme Court. A victory in those appeals would mean the remaining fourteen states that so far refused to permit or recognize the freedom to marry would have to both issue marriage licenses to same-sex couples and recognize same-sex marriages performed elsewhere. The favorable decision in a consolidated case was released two years to the day after *Windsor*. In the landmark case *Obergefell v. Hodges*, 135 S. Ct. 2584 (2015), the Court found:

> It is now clear that the challenged laws burden the liberty of same-sex couples, and it must be further acknowledged that they abridge central precepts of equality. Here the marriage laws enforced by the respondents are in essence unequal: same-sex couples are denied all the benefits afforded to opposite-sex couples and are barred from exercising a fundamental right. Especially against a long history of disapproval of their relationships, this denial to same-sex couples of the right to marry works a grave and continuing harm. The imposition of this disability on gays and lesbians serves to disrespect and subordinate them. (*Obergefell*, 22)

It was a sweeping nationwide victory for marriage equality. To read more about the case and the beautiful, heartbreaking story behind it, check out the recently published *Love Wins* by Jim Obergefell and Debbie Cenziper.

Implementing marriage equality is still a work in progress, especially in hostile regions. In some places, marriage, birth, and death certificates and form divorce pleadings have yet to change the terminology they use from "husband" and "wife" to "spouse." Those of us who remain focused on these issues will be busy for many years to come, ensuring that LGBT people are treated fairly and equitably under the law. For example, eight months after our marriage equality victory in Florida, we found ourselves back in federal court. This time we were suing the state's Department of Health, just as our colleagues in Texas and Utah had to do, over their refusal to issue birth certificates to children born to same-sex married couples on the same basis as different-sex married couples. Imagine this: legally married lesbians were giving birth in a state that recognized their marriage, but they were not being permitted to list their spouses on the birth certificates of their newborn babies. We knew from the rulings in Florida and at the U.S. Supreme Court that it is blatantly unconstitutional to treat our marriages any differently. Bizarrely enough, the Florida officials responsible for the issuance of birth certificates demanded clarification that the law applied to them, too. They got it in the form of yet another order compelling them to regard marriages between same-sex couples equally in all ways, including in the issuance of birth certificates to children born of our marriages.

We are far from done. We are still a nation without comprehensive federal discrimination protections in employment, public accommodations, or housing. Twenty-eight states do not explicitly prohibit firing someone because that person is gay or perceived to be gay, and thirty-two states do not explicitly prohibit firing someone because of that person's gender identity or gender expression. This is why you might have heard stories about LGBT people getting married only to get evicted or fired from their jobs afterward (as in the movie *Love Is Strange*, which tells the story of a long-term gay male couple who marry and, as a direct result, the spouse employed by a Catholic school gets fired). That a joyous celebration of love could be followed by loss of one's livelihood is almost too much to comprehend, but this represents the paradox of a movement that has come a long way on one discrete issue but still has far to go on much else.

It might seem that equality of marriage was achieved at the speed of light, but in fact it was a forty-five-year-long, painstaking battle fought in every corner of our nation: homes, universities, workplaces, houses of worship, hospitals, ballot boxes, legislatures, and courts. With this momentum and with the playbook forged by the victors of this battle, we will continue to fight to be free from all discrimination including that in housing, workplace, and public accommodations. We will use the winning combination of litigation, lobbying, and sharing our emotionally resonant truths to achieve justice for many others where issues other than marriage predominate: our youth, older adults, transgender people, and the many committed people who deserve protections but for whom marriage is not the answer.

3
STARTING OUT

Anything that's human is mentionable, and anything that is mentionable can be more manageable. When we can talk about our feelings, they become less overwhelming, less upsetting, and less scary.

—*Fred ("Mr.") Rogers*

Gay couples marry for the same reasons as straight couples: to express love and commitment in a way that is universally recognized. We seek stability; we want our relationships treated with the same dignity as heterosexual couples' relationships. We want a ritual to solemnize our promises to each other. We hope to be together for an eternity. We wish to feel safe and to make our beloved feel safe. We want to be bound to each other with more than a mortgage or bank account. We stand before family, friends, and community and pledge ourselves to each other, asking for the support of those around us to maintain that commitment should the path get rocky.

Before we get into the meaty legal aspects of marriage—what marriage means and doesn't mean from a legal perspective—it is worthwhile to determine whether you are going down this road with the right person, and what the road itself looks like.

ASKING EACH OTHER HARD QUESTIONS

Much as location, location, location is the secret to real estate success, communication, communication, communication is the key to a successful marriage. Family means different things to different people. Make sure you and your beloved are on the same page before you make a lifelong commitment. Get clear on the basics so that there will be fewer surprises later.

It is wise for couples to discuss the three big D's directly: death, disability, and divorce. What would happen in the event of any of these? To make this process less daunting, I have dug through the deal breakers in my divorce files and come up with some questions to discuss before taking the marital plunge.

1. Do you expect to keep your incomes and bank accounts separate or commingled?
2. What is your annual income? Do you anticipate stopping employment or asking the other spouse to do so as a consequence of marriage or having children?
3. Do you want children? If so, how do you imagine us having children? Are you open to adoption or assisted reproduction?
4. Do you believe in monogamy?
5. What are your assets? What do you own and where?
6. What kind of debt do you have? How much and to whom?
7. Have you ever been sued? Do you have any judgments against you?
8. Do you expect that a parent or other relative of yours would ever move in with us? Do you expect to provide financial or other support to a parent or relative?
9. How have your prior relationships ended? Would counseling have made a difference? Are you open to counseling?
10. Do you have any long-term health issues? What surgeries have you had? What medications are you on? Have you had or do you currently have any substance abuse issues?
11. Have you ever committed a crime? Been arrested? Served time in jail?
12. Are you current on your tax returns and payments?
13. Do you anticipate growing old in the town where we live now or do you hope to end up in a different setting?
14. What is your retirement plan? When do you plan to retire? What do you hope to do when you stop working?
15. Is there anyone else you want to provide for at your death?

Some conversations seem like they might be unnecessary. For example, how much does your soon-to-be spouse earn? You might think you have the income picture clear, but in this economy, which increasingly relies on independent contractors, the answer can be less than obvious. If your partner is a 1099 employee, you will want to have a chat about annual totals and fluctuations. These money-centric discussions can be awfully uncomfortable, but it is far worse not to have the conversations at all. It is better to have more than a general sense of how much money is coming in, how much money is spent and how, and how much is being set aside for retirement. I find that many of the healthiest couples I work with have a periodic sit-down to review these financial considerations. If you would rather stay in the dark than broach the topic, do so at your own peril.

Couples who are good communicators, who have these difficult conversations and memorialize their understandings in writing, are far less likely to separate. Maybe it has something to do with the willingness to broach difficult subjects, or maybe it's just luck. Still, it seems clear that those who have the courage to face these challenging topics do better in the long run.

WHAT DOES A CEREMONY MEAN TO YOU?

I am a lawyer, cautious by nature, and not a wedding planner, but I suggest not spending a ton of money on the whole wedding endeavor—unless you happen to have a ton of money and no other uses for it. A wedding does not have to be a Broadway production to be meaningful. One of the great stressors all couples face is debt. Weddings are expensive. Starting out married life worried about how much money you owe thanks to your wedding hoopla does not make for a happy beginning to a life together. Getting married should never compromise being married. If you do decide to go for a bigger soirée and have a limited budget, think about creative ways to save. Ask friends and family or find articles and books that give tips for a cost-conscious wedding. Have friends get together to create fun centerpieces and party favors. Be selective with the guest list. Or perhaps an elopement makes sense for you. There are plenty of folks who have been together for decades and their meaningful celebration was just the two of them at the courthouse.

Of course, weddings have a broader purpose than just the party or outfitting your home with new dishes and linens to start off a domestic life together. Part of the larger point of a wedding is to stand up in the presence of your loved ones as they bear witness to your vows and lifetime pledges to one another. The wedding ceremony brings families and communities together in a public affirmation of the relationship between the spouses. The Supreme Court of the United States was conscious of this and, in the *Windsor* decision, held that DOMA deprived same-sex couples of the fundamental right to "affirm their commitment to one another before their children, their family, their friends, and their community."

In a wedding, the couple asks for support from their community when times get tough. Especially in our transient society, having a broad network of friends and family can relieve your spouse of the pressure of being your sole source of support. No one person can be your "everything." Moreover, no marriage is without its challenges. The hope is that the people who attend your wedding will buttress the union when you hit a bumpy patch in the road. Either you or the officiant might announce that specific request during the ceremony, making the expectation clear that you hope your guests will help strengthen the relationship, not undermine it.

When planning your nuptials, consider how you will bring together biological family and chosen family to support and celebrate your union. This can be a delicate process, but when it is handled well it can be rewarding for everyone. Do not be afraid to color outside the lines while still respecting the traditions that are important to you. Give yourself license to reimagine some of the wedding rituals to best suit you and your bride or groom. For example, you might not both be lucky enough to have parents to walk you down the aisle. Consider giving that honor to a mentor or another dear soul who has been particularly supportive of you on your journey. Or maybe you would rather walk each other down the aisle instead, as a sign of your empowerment as a couple and as a break from the heterocentric and paternalistic convention that says a grown-up needs to be "given away."

SHOUT IT FROM THE ROOFTOPS

Announce your marriage! By having your marriage announced on social media sites or in the newsletters for your alma maters, religious institutions, and the like, you are being role models to other LGBT people, single or coupled, who still live with the fear of stigma. The freedom to marry does not instantly eliminate internalized homophobia like the flip of a switch. For many couples who have spent years calling our intended lifetime partners our "friends" or some other euphemism, it can be incredibly empowering to step into the sunshine and declare our love and commitment.

It is a great gift to your family and friends to give them the opportunity to come out themselves about their support of marriage equality. The value of educating hetero family and friends cannot be overestimated. I have long dreamed of having a source of funds to give grants for same-sex couples' weddings, especially those from cultures and places where invitees might be attending their first such celebration. Not only are even the most modest weddings expensive, but many times gay couples cannot rely on the tradition of having one family, or both, pay for the wedding. Reasons for that could include a lack of support or some combination of the age of the marrying couple and the number of years they have been together, which might make a wedding seem like an unnecessary indulgence. Most of the attendees tend to be hetero friends and family, and even if they are already on board with marriage equality (well, at least enough to show support by attending), they get a whole different and more profound view once they are a part of a same-sex couple's marriage celebration. It is the difference between intellectually believing and actually seeing. Marriage equality may now be the law of the land, but there is still resistance, largely among those who are less familiar with the LGBT community and our families. It would be great to be able to grant substantial amounts of money to engaged same-sex couples on limited budgets to throw meaningful celebrations inclusive of those in their broader circle of friends and family whom they might not otherwise be able to afford to invite. Until and unless that happens, my hope is that economically challenged brides and grooms do not compromise the financial viability of their marriage, but use creative ways to have a significant and sensible celebration while finding a way to broaden cultural acceptance of marriage equality.

The Unexpected Benefits of Marriage

CAROL BUELL

Attorney and mediator

Weiss, Buell & Bell

New York, New York

It's Saturday, June 24, 2011, and I am sitting in the waiting area of a car dealership in upstate New York while my car is being serviced. Just ten hours earlier, around midnight, the New York State Legislature passed a marriage equality bill, thanks to more people than I could possibly recognize. I am happy and amazed.

For some reason I don't yet understand, I pick up my cell phone, walk out of the dealership into the glorious June sunshine, and dial my partner's ninety-year-old mother in Little Rock, Arkansas. I've decided it is time to ask for her blessing to marry her daughter. As the phone rings, I picture her sitting in her small room at the Presbyterian assisted-living facility in which she lives. I imagine hearing her perfectly lovely Tennessee drawl when she picks up the phone. I imagine asking her this question . . . and I totally begin to panic! What if she says no? What if the blessing does not come?

I am fifty-six years old. Her daughter and I have been together for over thirty years. In the early 1980s we hid our relationship from our families. As the years sped by, we slowly "came out" to our siblings. Olivia was there by my side as I experienced the loss of my mother to breast cancer in the early 1990s. Together we began a nine-year journey from an idea of having a child together to the adoption of our daughter, born in Vietnam, in 2000. We eventually tell our parents about our relationship, and we share the loss of Olivia's father from Alzheimer's disease. And now her mother is a sharp nonagenarian and my father has beginning-stage Alzheimer's disease.

Over thirty years of family moments, but I realize in one split second, while the call is connecting, that there has never been an opportunity for us to ask this question. I realize I am not quite sure that I want to give her this much power. What was I thinking? I almost hang up the phone, but then I hear her perfect slow southern drawl. I let her know about the passage of marriage equality in New York the night before, and I tell her that I think it's about time I married her daughter. Would she give me her blessing?

"Well, I guess that would be all right," she says. We speak for a few more minutes before hanging up, and then I complete the circle by calling my father and asking him the same question. I think he understands, and he too gives his blessing.

I did not realize until now, when marriage is in my grasp, how important it is for me to hear those words from our parents. I felt their acceptance all these years—inclusion at family gatherings, an awareness and acceptance of our importance to each other—but I've never asked for nor received the blessings I so quickly understood would have to come if I am to marry Olivia. Such is the power of marriage. Who knew?

FIRST THINGS FIRST

If, after having all of the tough conversations and evaluating all of the factors discussed in this book, you still decide to take the plunge, here is your step-by-step guide to the big day.

Clear Up Other Statuses

The multiple statuses available to couples as we inched toward marriage mean that before you marry your beloved, you need to dissolve any other statuses entered into with others. Whether it is a civil union, a domestic partnership, or another kind of relationship status no longer recognized, it is critical to bring a formal end to it. Given the shifting sands that still exist around the bedrock of our relationships—and the homophobia that remains in many parts of the country—do not create confusion with multiple statuses with multiple people. Furthermore, there are bigamy laws! They make it a criminal offense to be married to two people at the same time. This applies to a marriage-equivalent status as well in any state that recognizes the status or may recognize it in the future. Do not risk this outcome. Take the dissolution of those other statuses seriously, even if that means a divorce proceeding in local family court. Ideally you will have already divided up any assets and debts from prior relationships so that you can have an uncontested, simple divorce.

There was a time when adoption felt to some same-sex couples like the only option to unite under the law. For younger LGBT people it might be hard to imagine a time like this, but a significant number of long-term same-sex couples have done adult adoptions, creating a parent-child relationship when that was the only kind of legal recognition that could exist between them. Folks did what they needed to do, and took advantage of the limited options available to them under the law at that time, motivated oftentimes by estate planning concerns. It is hard to know how many such adoptions happened, but each one speaks to how creative we were forced to be, while we were "outlaws," just to provide basic protections to our loved ones. These cases underscore why marriage equality was such an important victory for our community—it legitimized our relationships under the law without forcing us to jump through strange hoops.

If you adopted your partner, dissolve that legal relationship before you enter into marriage. Incest laws bar marriage with a legal parent, and in most states this includes an adoptive parent. While some states do permit marrying one's adoptive parent, do not risk being on the wrong side of the law. Adoption law varies by state; see an experienced adoption lawyer to investigate your options if you or your partner adopted the other. I have handled several adult adoptions that needed to be undone. In each case we were fortunate that the partners who were adopted had biological parents still alive, meaning that those biological parents could reestablish their legal relationships with their children through a second adoption. That later adoption had the effect of superseding the first adoption by the partner. The court order specifically stated that the partner's parental rights were terminated. This statement made the couple free to marry each other. In each case, I candidly explained to the court why the couple selected adoption in the past and why they wanted to terminate the adoption to be married. Judges were delighted to be able to help these long-term couples finally wed and enjoy the truest form of recognition for their relationship.

Couples who sought the remedy of adopting one another are often older. They might not have a surviving parent to do a new adoption, as my clients did. In such cases, investigate other options. Your state's laws might allow adults to simply terminate the parental rights of persons who are their legal parents either through birth or through adoption. Some might make the argument that these adoptions should just be vacated by the court. As an adoption lawyer, I want to be sure adoptions are safe and permanent; imagine birth moms who completed adoptions using such precedent to make the case that their circumstances have changed and they want their babies back. Therefore, I am leery of opening the door to simply setting aside adoptions.

Obtain a Marriage License

To get married, you need a marriage license and a ceremony. Whether choosing a civil or religious ceremony, couples must apply for a license, which the officiant and perhaps a witness will need to sign. The license needs to be returned to the issuing office within a certain number of days from issuance. In some states (Florida, Maine, and South Carolina), marriage can be solemnized by someone who is a notary public. The application process can sometimes begin online, but you will need to print out that completed application and bring it to your county clerk's office or whichever governmental entity issues the licenses. Marriage licenses usually require a fee of between $20 and $100. Both brides or both grooms need to appear in person with government-issued photo identification to apply for the license. Some states have waiting periods of a certain number of days between obtaining the license and having the officiant perform the ceremony and sign the license. In some places you can shorten that wait time by having taken a premarital course with an approved provider such as a counselor or clergyperson. Blood tests are still required in some places as well, presumably to prove you are not going to have children who will be exposed to some disease. If either of you has been married before, you could be required to prove that the marriage ended in death or divorce. Investigate the requirements of a marriage license where you live and give yourself time to secure one.

NAME CHANGE

Do you want to keep your own last name, take the other's name, hyphenate, or come up with an entirely new name (perhaps a blend of both surnames)? Think about that before marrying. Often you can simply indicate the intention to take your spouse's name on the marriage license by checking a box. In some places this can be more challenging for men since the system is not set up for that, but do not give up—it can be done.

It used to be a given that upon marriage, the wife would always take the husband's last name as part of being subsumed into his family. In fact, in some states a woman who did not take her husband's name could not vote or open a bank account. This tradition has become markedly less common among straight couples in recent decades, especially as people delay marrying until they are older and a woman's career and professional identity are already well established. For Angelina Jolie to have suddenly become Angelina Pitt would have obviously hurt her name recognition. Ironically, as same-sex couples are climbing aboard the institution, particularly those who are younger and less established in the working world, more and more are changing surnames just as our heterosexual counterparts are abandoning the practice.

If you simply seek to hyphenate or assume the other's name, you should be able to indicate that upon getting married by making that selection on the marriage license (also referred to as a marriage certificate). Then purchase multiple certified copies of your marriage license from the clerk who issued the license. "Certified" is a legal term for a copy that the clerk certifies is an exact duplicate of the original and therefore can serve in the stead of the original; they should cost just a few dollars each. Take those certified copies of the certificates to change your Social Security card, driver's license, passport, utilities, credit cards, and bank accounts. You will want to go roughly in that order, too, because once Social Security changes your name, the Department of Motor Vehicles and then the others will more easily fall into line. You can fill out the form SSA-5 (available at socialsecurity.gov) and either mail it in to the Social Security Administration or bring it in person to your nearest branch office.

You will not need to provide copies of the marriage certificate to all places where your name must be changed; some will allow you to make the change on the phone or online. Be thorough about changing everything to avoid problems later with names not matching. Remember to change your name with the Internal Revenue Service to avoid delay in processing any payments or refunds. The IRS form that you use to change a name, Form 8822, available at irs.gov, is titled "Change of Address," but it has a spot to indicate a new name as well. Tell your employer so that your paycheck will be accurate and you can deposit it into your bank account (which has changed to your current name). Folks sometimes forget about changing their names with doctors' offices. Remember to notify companies and institutions that do not send regular statements, such as frequent flyer accounts, insurance companies, the United States Postal Service, subscriptions, and store-specific credit card accounts. Also, any lenders or creditors, such as a mortgage company, student loan holder, or auto loan holder, will need to be informed to ensure that your credit history is accurate.

Typically, if you are coming up with an entirely new name, perhaps a hybrid of both spouses' surnames, that would need to be implemented in the courts through the formal name change process. The family division of your local county or circuit court handles name changes. It might require fingerprints and other background checks. Some states require publication, typically in a newspaper that runs legal notices in the back. The reason for all that is not to give you a hard time just for the fun of it, but rather to make sure that you are not changing your name for any nefarious motive, such as getting out of the payment of an outstanding judgment or avoiding a criminal charge. Many courts are moving toward providing greater self-help resources, making name change actions easy to handle pro se (without a lawyer). If your district or county has a website with the forms and instructions available online, you might be able to take care of it yourself with just the cost of the filing fee, usually several hundred dollars.

If you and your spouse married in a different jurisdiction earlier and then subsequently your marriage became recognized where you live, you may not have been allowed to do a name change upon marriage because either the federal government or your state government did not allow it using an out-of-state marriage certificate. It might still be possible to do a name change now without going through the formal name change process in the courts. Retrieve the physical marriage certificate and see if you indicated a request for a name change. If so, bring that to the Social Security Administration, Department of Motor Vehicles, and other places where you need to change your name. You might need to go back to the clerk's office for certified copies. Even if you did not select the name change option, try bringing it to the Social Security Administration office. Some states require that you change your name within a certain period of time after marriage, but you have a legitimate excuse if your marriage would not have triggered the ability to do the easy, free name change at home because of lack of recognition.

In the event of divorce, you can change your name back to your original surname in the divorce process by asking for the restoration of your name in your petition to the court. The divorce decree, or the final judgment of dissolution of marriage, should grant that relief and mention specifically that it restores your name. Get several certified copies of the divorce decree and present it to the relevant authorities mentioned previously.

NOTIFICATION ABOUT THE MARRIAGE

One question frequently asked is which entities need to be notified about your marriage. If you are changing your name, the work is more cumbersome. Otherwise, spread the word within the universes of Facebook, Twitter, Instagram, Snapchat, and whatever is the next big thing in social media.

Update your Form W-4 with your employer. This form, kept on file by your employer, determines the amount of taxes withheld from your pay. More taxes are withheld from your income if you are single than if you married. From an IRS perspective, it is not a requirement to change this form: just be sure that your actual tax filing at the end of the year is accurate and reflects your marriage status. Also, depending on whether your employer provides certain kinds of benefits, your marriage may be a "triggering event" that you need to disclose. Check with your company's human resources department if you feel comfortable doing so. If your workplace asks different-sex couples for proof of marriage, then you should expect that same requirement to apply to you.

Beware of the lack of clear, comprehensive nationwide employment discrimination protections. Many have reported informing their employers of their marriage to a person of the same gender and then being fired as a result. This action should be prohibited by federal law but this has not yet been clearly established, and it is not explicitly prohibited by state law in twenty-eight states. Do you live in a city or state that does not clearly prohibit your employer from firing you based on your sexual orientation or gender identity? If so, proceed with caution when announcing your wedding if you have reason to fear that your job may be on the line should you come out about your marriage. It is sad that such a concern needs to be a part of your celebration, but it does. The reality of the lack of employment protection serves as an important reminder that our LGBT rights movement still has much work to do.

There is no need to inform the Social Security Administration of your marriage unless you are receiving benefits already. When you are applying for benefits, you will be asked about marital status at that time.

If you are a service member or veteran, remember you will need to go to your Defense Enrollment Eligibility Reporting System (DEERS) office (see "Military Service" in Chapter 4) and prove your or your spouse's eligibility for those military benefits by showing your marriage certificate.

Oh, and just because people seem to ask this a lot: if you were married in another jurisdiction and your marriage later became recognized where you live, you need not marry again. Just as your parents might have married in Michigan and then moved to Illinois and did not remarry upon relocating, you need not, either.

4
WHAT MARRIAGE MEANS

Keep your eyes wide open before marriage, half shut afterwards.

—*Ben Franklin*

Marriage is as old as the hills, but gay men and lesbians are novices at nuptials. Becoming informed about the myriad implications of marriage is important. Marriage is an act of faith. "'Til death do us part" is a beautiful aspiration. What is the reality? Marriage provides protections—and creates obligations.

From a legal perspective, marriage is a business transaction. With it, two people get federal, state, and societal benefits. Marriage is a binding legal contract. Romance aside, when you examine the implications of marriage in light of your particular circumstances, there can be as many, if not more, reasons *not* to marry as there are reasons *to* marry.

Marriage can provide a host of protections for us and our families, but it can also jeopardize protections already in place. None of the following should be taken as an argument not to wed; it is simply information about what to expect. No one likes unpleasant surprises.

TAXES

Income Taxes: Bonuses + Penalties = Equality

When you marry, you must file income tax returns as a married person, such that your spouse's income and deductions can impact your taxes. There are two options: married filing separately and married filing jointly. Depending on your circumstances, income taxes create one of the major benefits or liabilities of marriage. Whether you marry someone in a different tax bracket or your own tax bracket, marriage can mean either a major tax liability, referred to as a marriage penalty, or a big tax savings, known as a marriage bonus. Everyone's tax situation is different; consulting with an accountant or tax preparer prior to marriage is prudent.

As a general rule, when a couple has a substantial income disparity, they will enjoy a marriage bonus, but when the incomes are about the same, whether they are high earners or low earners, the dreaded marriage penalty can rear its ugly head. Married couples report their combined incomes, even if those incomes are maintained in separate accounts, to the IRS. Couples can end up paying more income tax and losing certain deductions and credits. To those folks, marriage, from a tax perspective, is not all sunshine and rainbows. My mantra to those frustrated couples is: welcome to equality!

Often when I address groups and the heterosexual members of the audience hear me suggest considering potential tax penalties for marrying, they snicker. They never consulted with an accountant before marrying; how unromantic to do so. My reply? Maybe they should have! For a high-earning couple, the tax hit is too big to ignore and at least deserves consideration.

William and Alan's Story

••••••••••••••

William and Alan, a loving and committed couple, have been queer activists for many years. Always very politically oriented, they felt that marriage was a heteronormative bourgeois institution for which they had no use. They lamented the mainstreaming of the gay community and resented the expectation that all couples want to be monogamous marrieds with kids. Having been together for two decades, they did not feel a piece of paper would make their relationship any deeper or more enduring. They were so proud of living outside the law that they did not even create an estate plan. They thought, why bother wasting money on estate planning when its documents are not always respected when they need to be? Besides, they thought, what could a lawyer write about their relationship that they did not already feel themselves?

Then Alan suffers a heart attack. When he goes to the emergency room, William is prevented from visiting him in the hospital or making medical decisions for him. Luckily, Alan recovers. When he leaves the hospital, William and Alan decide to marry lickety-split. As newlyweds, they are excited to reap the benefits of their marital status. After getting their car insurance discount for married couples, they drive over to their CPA's office for what they are hoping is more good news. With bonuses, William earns about $175,000 annually. Alan's salary is $150,000 per year. When they file their taxes, they are shocked to learn that the federal government congratulates them on their marriage by slapping them with an additional $5,000 in income taxes. That is a marriage penalty.

The marriage penalty means that a couple may pay more income tax as a married couple than as single individuals. This structure is in place because tax laws originally contemplated one income-earning spouse and one non-income or low-income-earning spouse serving as a stay-at-home parent. Even if you are not big earners, you could end up paying a bigger income tax bill once you are married because you are now collectively bigger earners. The marriage penalty usually is triggered when there are similar incomes for both spouses, moving them together into a higher tax bracket, or a spouse who was paying minimal taxes on a low income now having her income added to the income of her spouse and being kicked into a higher tax bracket.

When there is a sizable disparity in earnings, marriage could be a benefit. The overall tax bracket of the married couple is often lower than the higher-earning spouse's tax bracket as a single filer. There are enhanced tax deductions and credits for which only married couples qualify. Certain deductions increase for married couples, such as the exclusion on the capital gains from the sale of a house and the mortgage interest deduction. The standard deduction is fully double for a married couple: $6,300 for individuals and $12,600 for married couples filing jointly. Married couples can deduct more charitable contributions. Depending on income and whether you and/or your spouse have employer-sponsored retirement plans, a working spouse can make IRA contributions (and deduct them on the joint tax return) for a nonworking spouse. These tax treatments can offer substantial savings for married couples.

Bruce and Miguel's Story

....

The year they marry, Bruce's earnings are $130,000 and Miguel, who was not legally able to work because of immigration issues, earned $28,000 building websites and doing graphic design for friends and acquaintances. Of all the people congratulating them on their union, none was happier for them than their accountant; she was able to save them approximately $2,840 in income taxes. Their marital status and Miguel's lower income brought Bruce down from a higher tax bracket, making his tax liability lower. In addition, once they married, Miguel qualified for a green card and became eligible for different employment opportunities. Different employment has different tax consequences. Bruce and Miguel, with their accountant, run the prospective numbers. Some jobs change their tax bonus to a substantial tax liability because of the increase in their household income. They have to consider whether it is worth it for Miguel to take on the higher paid work. Bruce and Miguel also discuss with a corporate lawyer whether they should set up a family partnership for Bruce's freelance business, which allows them, as a married couple, to spread out earnings between them in a tax-advantageous way.

Any couple thinking about marriage should discuss the implications first with a tax preparer. At the very least, check out one of the marriage penalty or bonus tax calculators online, such as the excellent one from the Tax Policy Center at http://taxpolicycenter.org/taxfacts/marriagepenaltycalculator.cfm. There can be great rewards for being proactive in seeking out this information.

MARRIAGE'S EFFECT ON INCOME TAXES: BONUS OR PENALTY?

Bruce and Miguel's marriage gives Miguel opportunities to increase his income. But depending on his earnings, this could result in a tax bonus or a tax penalty.

Joint income	Bruce's tax bill (filing single)	Miguel's tax bill (filing single)	Total tax bill (filing single)	Total tax bill (married filing jointly)	Difference
$158,000	$26,594	$2,198	$28,792	$25,944	–$2,848
$168,000	$26,594	$3,698	$30,292	$28,444	–$1,848
$178,000	$26,594	$5,225	$31,819	$31,131	–$688
$188,000	$26,594	$7,725	$34,319	$33,931	–$388
$198,000	$26,594	$10,225	$36,819	$36,731	–$88
$208,000	$26,594	$12,725	$39,319	$39,531	$212
$218,000	$26,594	$15,525	$42,119	$42,331	$212
$228,000	$26,594	$17,725	$44,319	$45,131	$812
$238,000	$26,594	$20,434	$47,028	$47,931	$903
$248,000	$26,594	$23,234	$49,828	$50,731	$903
$258,000	$26,594	$26,034	$52,628	$53,879	$1,251

Calculated using standard deduction and exemption for each party.

Tania and Marie's Story

•••••••••••

Tania and Marie were wise enough to see an accountant before they married. Tania works for her family's bodega and takes a small salary. Marie is *a teacher. They knew they wanted to be parents and that one of them could stay at home to focus on raising their child. They thought it best to explore the tax effects of marriage and if, once there was a child in the picture, it would make sense for Tania to stop working in the bodega and take a few years to be at home with their offspring. Marie's income as a teacher was $50,000. Tania usually declared around $15,000. If they married, there would be a marriage bonus of $450. If Tania stopped working when they got married, there would be a marriage bonus of about $2,250. The arrival of a child would cause the numbers to shift. If Tania and Marie married and Tania continued working at the bodega, they would have to spend about $10,000 per year for child care. As a result, they would get hit with a marriage penalty of $2,200, while a decision for her to stay at home caring for the child would mean no child care costs and a marriage bonus of $2,850. These are eye-opening calculations. Beyond the math, the consequences of this decision for Tania to stay home should be thoroughly thought through. What happens if they split up and she needs to make it on her own? What if her parents no longer own the bodega? Could she find a job after being out of the workforce for a number of years?*

If you decide to marry, talk to an accountant about these tax issues. Long-term couples can also see if there are income tax returns or gift tax returns already filed that could be amended retroactively.

I Do, Mr. Taxman: How Marital Status Can Impact Your Taxes

KAREN STOGDILL

Tax preparer/enrolled agent

San Francisco, California, and Fort Myers, Florida

After a seminar on tax issues for couples considering marriage, a young couple approached me saying, "We must have the simplest circumstances of all the couples here. One of us just graduated from college and has an entry-level job, and the other one is still in school and only works in the summer. Is it safe to assume our getting married will not impact our federal taxes much?"

While on the face of it this seems logical—in fact, one of the specific points in the seminar was that if one spouse is earning most of the money, it's likely the couple will pay less federal income tax overall—in this particular circumstance the lower-earning partner would actually lose education credits that she was entitled to as a single filer because now the income from both spouses would be considered. I projected that their federal income tax would increase by $3,000, a huge percentage increase for them.

Broad generalizations are very hard to make with respect to federal taxation and marital status. Some couples will save a significant amount of tax upon marrying, while other couples will actually see a large increase in their federal tax liability. Some will see very little change. This is true for both same-sex couples and different-sex couples who marry.

In 2015 the Internal Revenue Code stood at 74,608 single-spaced pages. These pages contain the rules you must follow to determine both your annual federal income taxes and any inheritance taxes due at your death. It also covers taxation rules relating to divorce and gifts of property—for example, if you want to add your partner to your house title. The rules are complex and often seemingly contradictory; Congress also changes them frequently.

There are many federal marriage tax benefits as well as many federal marriage tax penalties. Your bottom line will depend on your specific circumstances for that specific year. If the couple mentioned above married, they would pay substantially more federal income tax while the partner is still in school. But depending on their income levels after graduation, they may save federal taxes each year thereafter by being married.

What tax professionals working with the gay community have discovered is that individual circumstances determine the outcome. So while we cannot make broad generalizations about who will or will not save federal taxes by marrying, we can point out myriad tax penalties and tax benefits that may be affected by your change in marital status.

So what should you consider if contemplating marriage and you want to understand its impact on your federal income taxes?

Your filing status will change. If you marry at any point during a calendar year, including on December 31, your tax filing status changes to married for the entire tax year. Previously you would probably have filed either as a single taxpayer or possibly as head of household if you have children. Going from single to married status may or may not increase your federal taxes. Generally, going from filing as head of household to filing as married will almost certainly increase your federal tax significantly because you will lose this special tax break.

The tax table used to calculate your tax will change. The tax tables used to calculate tax for married couples are not simply the single tax tables times two. Generally the tax code was structured to benefit couples with a breadwinning spouse and a stay-at-home spouse.

Your income limits will change. There are many, many tax breaks that are dependent on the taxpayer's total amount of income—for example, the amount of medical expenses you can deduct, the amount of total miscellaneous itemized deductions you are allowed, the ability to deduct rental losses, whether or not you are allowed to make an IRA contribution, how much of your Social Security benefits are taxable, and so on. All items that have an earnings test could be affected by a change in marital status because now you are combining your two incomes. But the limits for married couples for tax deductions or tax credits are not always (in fact, rarely are) twice the single limit.

Your alternatives will change. One obvious question, then, is "Why don't we file as married filing separately?" While it is something to contemplate, unfortunately the married-filing-separately status rarely results in tax savings, although it may result in reduced legal liability. When you sign a joint tax return you are attesting that all of the information in the return is accurate. If your spouse has a complex tax situation and you have little to no knowledge about the specifics, you might consider the liability you are assuming by signing a joint tax return. In some circumstances choosing the married-filing-separately status is more prudent. Also, in community property states such as California that also have an option of registering as domestic partners instead of marrying, you could save significant federal taxes by being registered domestic partners instead of spouses. My tax practice has saved clients hundreds of thousands of dollars by having them file as single under the community property rules. But you should consult an expert to be sure you understand the pros and cons.

These are some of the federal income tax impacts to consider, but don't forget that *United States v. Windsor* was a case about estate taxes, not income taxes. If it is possible that you will have a taxable estate at death, you should consult with an estate tax attorney as well. By having her marriage to Thea Speyer recognized federally, Edie Windsor saved more than $300,000 in federal estate taxes upon Thea's death.

Also remember that even if you are not considering the emotional, societal, or other legal aspects of marriage, only the financial questions, the financial impact is not limited to your federal income, estate, and gift tax liabilities. Your marital status will also affect both your access to and the dollar amount of other benefits that you may be eligible to receive, including Social Security (both retirement and disability benefits), Medicare, and Medicaid. There may also be financial impacts based on your state of residence.

It is wise to remember that in our society your marital status has significant and wide-ranging implications. Consulting an attorney familiar with specific LGBT issues is always recommended, as a qualified attorney can offer sage advice and can quarterback a team of professionals appropriate to your particular situation, including family law specialists, tax professionals, estate experts, social benefit advisors, and others.

While it is probably true that most marrying couples primarily consider the emotional and societal benefits of marriage, it is prudent to also look at legal and financial implications that could significantly benefit or hinder your family. Taxes are certainly one of those.

OTHER INCOME TAX ISSUES

Adoption Tax Credit

The adoption tax credit is substantial and offsets not only the costs of adopting a child unrelated to you or your partner but also the costs of a second-parent adoption, which is when you adopt a child who legally belongs to your partner by birth or adoption. There is an important caveat regarding second-parent adoptions, however: couples cannot take the adoption tax credit for a second-parent adoption if they are married, because then it is considered a stepparent adoption, and the credit is not available for adopting your spouse's child. Some LGBT parents complete a second-parent adoption and then marry afterwards to maximize the tax benefits of both in that year. Making this choice, however, means you do not have the benefit of the marital presumption of parentage from birth, and are more vulnerable in many states until the adoption is completed. Note that this is an exception to the usual IRS rule that if you are married at any point during the year, you are considered married for the whole year for tax purposes.

Dependents

A taxpayer's spouse cannot be a dependent of the taxpayer, and for some couples the dependent benefit is better than the benefit that can be obtained by filing jointly. If your partner does not work, talk to your tax advisor to see if she is eligible as a dependent for tax purposes—that may be more tax-advantageous than marriage.

Earned Income Tax Credit

The earned income tax credit (EITC) is designed to help low- and moderate-income families. The credit provides a dollar-for-dollar reduction in the amount of tax due, and if no tax is due, the credit is refunded in the form of a check sent to the eligible taxpayer. The amount of the credit varies based on income, filing status, and whether you have children. For example, for a parent with one qualifying child to be able to file for the EITC in 2016, the parent's income must be less than $39,296, or $44,846 if married filing jointly, in order to receive a $3,373 tax credit. To qualify for EITC purposes, a child can be a biological or adopted child, a stepchild, a foster child, a minor sibling, or the child of any of these, such as a grandchild. Depending on your spouse's income, marriage could increase or decrease your tax credit. The credit is phased out (that is, it decreases and then ends) as income increases. Other couples might see a larger credit upon marriage based upon a change in the amount of combined taxable income and the number of children.

Alternative Minimum Tax (AMT)

Congress created the AMT to capture revenue from wealthy taxpayers whose many deductions resulted in their paying less income tax and even no income tax whatsoever. Higher-earning couples who wed might learn that they have a higher tax bracket due to the inclusion of the second income and could face the alternative minimum tax as well.

INSURANCE

Insurance coverage is important. All married couples should be able to add spouses to employer-provided health insurance plans. If different-sex married couples are eligible for inclusion under a workplace group policy, same-sex married couples are as well. When we were searching for plaintiffs to launch our litigation effort to overturn the Florida marriage ban, this was one of the most common complaints we heard from same-sex couples anxious for statewide marriage equality. They were being told that until the state ban was lifted, employers and private health insurance companies could not be forced to provide equal access to group insurance plans. Those days are over.

Also over are the days when we would have to pay income tax on the amount spent to cover our partner under our employer-provided health insurance. Unless we remain unmarried and continue coverage for a registered domestic partner, the dollar value of employer-provided spousal coverage is no longer considered taxable income for the employee. Many couples had an experience similar to mine: for ten years before we married, my wife, then an employee of a major metropolitan newspaper owned by a national parent company, covered me on her health insurance as her domestic partner. Because we were not a heterosexual married couple, the cost of my health insurance was treated as taxable income for her. We paid approximately $1,100 in taxes each year on my health benefits. Once we married, we were eligible for coverage tax-free.

Other types of insurance are more affordable as well. I shopped for long-term care insurance both before I got married and then again after, and discovered that I qualified for a lower premium after I was married. There is actuarial proof that we are healthier as we age if we are married. That means that, as a group, married people are cheaper to cover since we utilize the policies less.

If you marry, call up your automobile insurer and see if you qualify for a discount. Apparently many companies determine that you are somehow deemed a less risky driver once married; that ought to translate into lower premiums on your car insurance. If you do not get this discount from your insurer, consider shopping around and giving the business to another company. You might be surprised at the cost savings.

If you are insured under the Affordable Care Act (also known as Obamacare), you are likely receiving a stipend to help subsidize your health insurance costs. Upon marrying, you might get a lower stipend, if any at all. Here is where there is another "marriage penalty." An individual can earn roughly $46,000 and still be eligible for a reduction in premium. Upon marrying, the maximum amount that the couple can earn is approximately $62,000; over that household income, no subsidies are available. Insured couples with high deductible plans offered on the marketplace might suffer from a marriage penalty because the deductible for a family is higher than for an individual. For example, a couple that has separate plans, each with a deductible of $2,000, might get married and find that the same plan now comes with a "family" deductible of $5,000, meaning they would pay an extra $1,000 out-of-pocket before the plan's coverage kicks in.

A note about Tricare, the health insurance program for military service members, veterans, and their families. In several cases marriage causes those benefits to end. If you were eligible for Tricare coverage because of your spouse's service and then you divorce or your spouse dies, you can retain Tricare until you remarry. If you are the service member from whom the Tricare eligibility stems, your ex-spouse retains his Tricare benefits unless he remarries. The same goes for a young adult (under age twenty-six) using her parent's Tricare: when she marries, her eligibility terminates.

COBRA

The Consolidated Omnibus Budget Reconciliation Act (COBRA) is how an employee can retain group health insurance benefits for himself and his family for a specified amount of time after resigning or being terminated from his job. An employer does not have to provide this benefit to your boyfriend or girlfriend, but if your married partner leaves his job, the employer has no choice: you are legally entitled to keep the group health insurance coverage through COBRA for approximately thirty-six months by paying the cost the employer was paying plus an administrative premium.

Federal/State Employee Benefits

A great benefit of marriage for employees of state or federal government is the ability to extend some of your work-related benefits to your spouse. Oftentimes these benefits are both substantial and available only to legally wedded spouses. Some benefits, such as Federal Employee Group Life Insurance (FEGLI), have been made available to domestic partners in addition to spouses, but many others require a marriage for eligibility.

Check with your Employee Assistance Program office for specific benefits available, and ask whether using them has consequences. Typically, state and federal workers may designate their same-sex spouse as the beneficiary for benefits at the death of the employee and may enroll her in health insurance through the Federal Employees Health Benefits Program or state equivalent thereof. The good news is you will not have to pay income tax on that benefit and the insurance premium savings are frequently huge. To add your spouse to your health, dental, and vision insurance benefits, inform the Office of Personnel Management, which administers the many benefits available to federal government workers and retirees, anytime from a month before to two months after the date of marriage.

You might, however, see some reduction in benefits yourself if you make certain beneficiary designations for your spouse. For example, if you are a pension-eligible federal government employee and add a death benefit so that your surviving spouse receives a lump sum at your death, your annuity (the annual amount you receive as a pension during your life) is reduced. This beneficiary designation is not automatic upon marriage but rather is an election that you have the option of making within two years of marriage. The reduction in your annuity can be substantial. The reduction amount is different depending on whether you married before or after retirement. If you are a current federal government employee, you are subject to the Civil Service Retirement System, and if you are a retired federal government employee, it is the Federal Employee Retirement System. Either way, for more details about what the adding of a spousal benefit would mean to you, write to the Office of Personnel Management and send in a copy of your marriage certificate showing the date of the marriage. You will then receive information about the cost of the benefit. Fear not—you will be asked to confirm your election before making a final decision, so after you learn what the amount would be, you can still change your mind and not enroll your spouse for that particular benefit.

If you work for the federal or state government either as an employee or as a contractor, be sure to review the section "Governmental Employees and Contractors Ethics Standards" later in this chapter. It discusses conflict-of-interest rules and how marriage will impact your disclosure obligations under the strict ethics standards.

DEBT

Marriage affects money we might owe or might think about borrowing in the future. The rules differ somewhat whether you are in a community property state or not. When you marry in a community property state, the debt incurred by either spouse in the marriage is deemed a debt of the couple, while in the rest of the nation, known as common-law states (not to be confused with the states that recognize common-law marriage, as we will discuss in Chapter 12), that debt can remain separate if handled properly.

Credit Reports

Getting married will not automatically impact your credit report. You each maintain your own credit, which is associated with your Social Security number. If you change your name upon marriage, the new name is automatically reflected on your existing credit report; the old credit history is not wiped away. On the upside, if you are marrying someone with a low credit score, it will not bring your score down. Your hubby's poor score will, however, impact you when you try to purchase a home, car, or anything else for which you jointly apply for financing. Both credit reports will be pulled before you can be allowed to cosign for debt, and the loan's interest rate might be higher or you can be denied the loan altogether because of the risk of lending money to the spouse with the bad credit history. It might be wiser to apply for the loan in the name of the spouse with the higher credit score to secure a better monthly payment.

Credit Cards

One of the many repeated points of misunderstanding among people I consult with is assuming that giving someone your credit card to use means that what is spent is not your debt. When you allow someone else, a spouse or a boyfriend or whomever, to use your card, any debts that person incurs are with your authorization and therefore are attributable to your Social Security number. If you apply for a card together with someone, married or not, that card will be connected to both Social Security numbers and therefore both cosigners are equally responsible for the debt. If you are married and your spouse incurs credit card debt in his own name, even if the credit card company cannot go after you personally, the debt may be included in a divorce and you are still responsible for half. This is true whether the expenses were for household use or for the personal gain of only one spouse.

Judgments

Being married and having your assets held jointly can be a good thing if you get sued. Judgment creditors cannot go after property that is jointly owned by a married couple as tenants by the entireties unless the debt involved was incurred by both of you. As we learn later in the section "Property Ownership," it is much more difficult for a creditor of one spouse to attach property held by both as tenants by the entireties (unless the creditor is the IRS). If you marry someone with a judgment against her, you do not become responsible for that obligation by virtue of the marriage.

Student Loans

Most schools, especially state schools, use the Free Application for Federal Student Aid (FAFSA) to determine a student's available resources and thus her eligibility for financial assistance. If you are married and looking for aid to go to school, you must report the income of your spouse.

In order to obtain a student loan, you must list both parents' incomes, whether they are a same-sex or different-sex couple, whether they live together, whether they are married or not, or if they do not live together but are both legal parents (through an adoption or some other court process declaring them both parents). If you and your partner have a child together and you are both legal parents of that child, do not think that not being married will save you having to include financial information for both parents. You will need to answer the FAFSA questions for both legal parents. If you have a child and only one of you is the legal parent, however, even if you live together and your partner is supporting the child for whom he has no parental rights, there is no need to report his financial information.

If you marry someone with student loans (or any other kind of debt, for that matter), that debt does not become your debt. Only if you cosign for the loan with your spouse would you become responsible for that debt. Exercise caution when making the decision to guarantee a loan. Consider also that if you are marrying someone with debt, while that debt does not become yours, you are entering into a marriage with someone who has a limited capacity to take on more debt and may never qualify for a mortgage or a car loan. Marriage should generally enhance your ability to borrow. With limited credit, together you might not be able to take out loans that help you build a better future.

Injured Spouse Allocation

Your spouse's prior federal or state tax liabilities do not become your debts upon marriage. If, however, you marry someone with outstanding debt to the IRS or state taxing authority, or someone who is in arrears with his student loans or child or spousal support payments, it is possible that your tax refund could be seized and applied to those outstanding amounts. If your spouse owes child support, money seized by the IRS goes to the child; otherwise, seized tax refunds apply to other outstanding debts. If this is an issue for you and you have not yet married, consider what exposure you might be taking on by marrying; it might be substantial if you rely on your tax refund each year. If you are already married, see a tax professional about assisting you with an Injured Spouse Allocation (IRS Form 8379). This form initiates a procedure to get a portion of your refund returned. The amount you are able to recover is not necessarily half but rather is calculated based on the amount of the total refund that is attributable to your individual income. If you are affected by this circumstance, you must file the Injured Spouse Allocation each year that you expect the outstanding amount due to result in an offset of your refund. The form can be submitted either in anticipation of a refund being co-opted or afterward. If you live in a community property state (see the "Bankruptcy" section that follows for a list of community property states), the option to obtain this relief is limited because tax refunds are deemed joint property and not subject to the same allocation rules.

Bankruptcy

Marriage can be a good or bad thing from a bankruptcy perspective. If your debt is joint, then being married means you can file a joint petition, saving a second filing fee and likely some legal fees as well. One action is less costly than two. Joint debt includes a credit card that was issued in both names even if you never used it or charged a single item. You would likely want to file jointly for marital debt in order to protect both individuals: if you filed singly, the spouse who does not file would remain exposed to the claims of creditors instead of being included in the deal worked out with creditors and then being shielded from further collection efforts.

There are two main types of bankruptcy proceedings: Chapter 7 and Chapter 13. Chapter 7 results in those debts being completely eliminated after any eligible assets (those not exempt from liquidation) are sold to pay creditors. What constitutes an exempt asset varies by state, but usually you can keep your home and some personal property. To qualify for Chapter 7, you have to pass a means test in which you prove that your income does not exceed a certain level relative to the average of others where you live.

Chapter 13 is less forgiving. Through a Chapter 13 proceeding, a court helps you work out a payment plan to satisfy a portion of your debts after your nonexempt property is sold. Both forms of bankruptcy have negative effects on your credit, and the bankruptcy judgment remains on your credit report for up to ten years. Make sure you are not trying to get rid of manageable debt. Also, note that there are certain very common kinds of debt that cannot be gotten rid of, including taxes owed to the federal government, alimony and child support, and student loans.

In some states, the amount of property a married couple can consider exempt is double that of an individual. However, it can be

COMMUNITY PROPERTY STATES

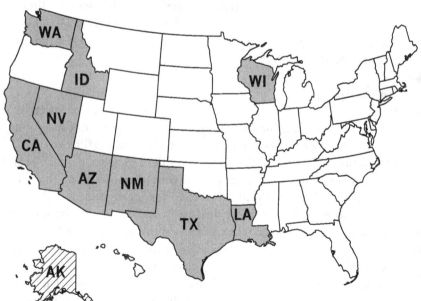

Alaska allows both spouses to elect whether their assets will be considered community property.

harder to qualify for the more desirable Chapter 7 (which is the one that completely discharges the debt, as opposed to paying off the agreed-upon amount in installments) if you are married because both spouses' incomes are considered for the means test.

If just one spouse is in debt, you would not want to file jointly and implicate the credit and property of the other spouse. Unless your spouse cosigned a loan for you before you married, she is not implicated in any debt you incurred before marriage. If the spouse who is not filing has assets in her name alone, those assets are not part of the bankruptcy estate and need not be sold to repay creditors.

The outcome of bankruptcy can vary in community property states, where you might need to prove that the individual asset is in fact not an asset of the marriage and therefore is exempt from the bankruptcy proceeding. Community property states (Arizona, California, Idaho, Louisiana, Nevada, New Mexico, Texas, Washington, and Wisconsin) consider all premarital debt (and assets) to be assumed by your spouse at the time of marriage; it gets difficult to prove what is nonmarital. There are agreements that can be entered into before marriage in community property states whereby assets and debts do not become transmuted (converted) into community assets.

As with other issues discussed in this book generally and this chapter specifically, bankruptcy is a factor to be considered by gay and straight couples alike. Marrying someone who has filed for bankruptcy is an extra reason to proceed with caution in merging accounts and potentially exposing your credit score to your spouse's poor spending habits. (Again, you do not merge credit scores when marrying: each person retains his own credit score. But when you get joint credit cards and he gets a little too spendy, that is when your credit score suffers.) There might be issues buying a home or a car together because of your spouse's poor credit. You might want to think twice before cosigning on a loan with your spouse if she has filed for bankruptcy, because a default could result in creditors coming after you first—since without your signature the loan likely would not have been issued in the first place.

If you find yourself with debt so large that you reasonably believe you will not be able to pay it off, consult with a bankruptcy lawyer. She can review options to discharge debt as a last resort. Should you find yourself partnered with someone who has filed bankruptcy, ask lots of questions about the circumstances. If there appears to be a pattern of bad financial judgments, it might be unwise to commingle assets. Again and again, I repeat: look before you leap.

SOCIAL SECURITY PROGRAMS

Ever wonder why your grandma and her "gentleman friend" are intentionally *not* getting married? It may not be just because they are trying to keep their romantic options open at the retirement home. They might be purposely maximizing the retirement benefits they receive. Married individuals generally receive less together than they did as unmarried individuals, under the theory that two can live more cheaply than one. It is also possible that your grandmother is claiming the Social Security benefit of your grandfather, if they were married for more than ten years and his benefits exceeded hers. If you are on a benefits program that determines your subsidy by looking at what resources you have available, you need to be aware of the so-called marriage penalty. No one is suggesting gaming the system or cheating the government here. Rather, be aware of the consequences of marrying, and plan your budget accordingly.

Social Security is the fruit of our lifetime of labor. Generally, individuals can collect Social Security at different times in life: at retirement, when a parent dies leaving a dependent child, at the retirement of a spouse, at the death of a spouse or former spouse, or upon becoming disabled. The amount paid is based on your own work history or that of a spouse or parent. The Social Security administration calls the primary eligible person a "number holder" or a "worker," and that person must have enough credits to be eligible. Currently each credit represents $1,220 in wages, with a maximum of four credits attainable per year; forty credits earns you eligibility unless you are disabled or collecting as a child of an eligible worker.

Marriage impacts Social Security in a variety of ways. Marriage increases or decreases Social Security benefit payments depending on how you are eligible for the benefit. If you are eligible for Social Security, you will be able to collect a greater amount of benefits if your spouse's retirement benefits are 150 percent or more of yours. In other words, if your spouse is eligible for $2,200 in monthly Social Security benefits and your benefits only amount to $800, you can elect to receive a total benefit of $1,100 instead of your $800. You must be married for one year to collect benefits based on your marriage if the number holder is alive and nine months if the number holder is deceased. The Social Security Administration has also been willing to consider the length of what they call nonmarital legal relationships or stack them with marriages to arrive at the duration requirements. Nonmarital legal relationships include civil unions, domestic partnerships, and the lesser statuses of designated and reciprocal beneficiaries that some states also recognize. They will count for Social Security benefits purposes provided those relationships were recognized in the number holder's state of domicile and if the survivor would be entitled to automatic inheritance rights based on that relationship status.

For many same-sex couples, entitlement to spousal retirement or survivor benefits is a major reason for marriage, but for countless couples this relief came too late: the number holder or worker spouse had already passed away or was too infirm to wed. Fortunately, the Social Security Administration has been willing to grant retroactive benefits to any otherwise eligible person who was in a same-sex marriage and had filed for those benefits even before their home state recognized their marriage. These benefits are only paid if the couple had been married for at least nine months before the deceased spouse passed away, which has left many surviving LGBT spouses, unable to marry sooner, without this critical benefit.

Determining the benefit amount you will be entitled to receive at retirement or at the death of a spouse is important. In the past, the Social Security Administration mailed out annual statements reflecting lifetime annual incomes and monthly Social Security payments at retirement. These statements are now mailed at certain intervals depending on your age and whether you have logged in and created an account at socialsecurity.gov. It is wise to log in and verify that the annual income listed is accurate; if not, correct it. Knowing the amount of your Social Security benefits can help you determine how much to save to supplement those benefits and when you could plan to retire.

If you work until full retirement age (age sixty-seven if you were born in or after 1960; age sixty-six if you were born in 1959 or before), you receive your full benefit amount. You can retire as early as age sixty-two, but if you retire before full retirement age your annual benefit is reduced; it does not increase when you reach full retirement age. If you delay retiring beyond full retirement age, the amount you collect is steadily increased up until age seventy.

Widow(er) Receiving Social Security

If you lose a spouse before you turn sixty (or before fifty if you are disabled), you are entitled to receive Social Security benefits for being a widow(er) but will lose them if you remarry before age sixty. You do not forfeit the benefits you are collecting based on your former spouse's work record if you remarry after reaching age sixty unless you elect the spousal allowance you might be eligible for with your new spouse.

You receive a one-time payment of $255 at the death of your spouse if she had enough credits. Benefits paid to a disabled widow(er) based on her own work record are unaffected by remarriage; if you are already receiving Social Security benefits based on your own age eligibility, your own work history, and your own health, getting married will not affect those payments.

If you are the biological or adoptive parent of a deceased worker's child who is younger than sixteen or disabled, you can collect on the worker's benefits at any age to assist with the care of that child. In some cases you can also collect when caring for a dependent child or stepchild with whom you have no biological or adoptive connection.

To decide whether you would do better collecting on your own Social Security benefits or those of your spouse, check your estimated benefit at socialsecurity.gov. In general, if your deceased spouse's benefit is more than twice yours, you can elect to receive her benefit instead of yours. If you are receiving benefits as a surviving spouse before your full retirement age and the retirement benefits based on your work record are higher, you can switch to your own benefits as early as age sixty-two. Remember the marriage and/or nonmarital legal relationship duration requirement for a surviving spouse to collect: nine months.

Remember Alan and William (introduced earlier in this chapter), who eloped after Alan's hospital scare? After thirty years together and a year married, Alan passed away. His Social Security benefit was $2,500 per month, and William's is $1,100. William can elect to receive Alan's Social Security benefit of $2,500 instead of his $1,100.

Divorced Person Receiving Social Security

If you divorce after being married legally for ten years, and then your ex-spouse dies, you might be eligible to receive benefits based on your former spouse's work record once you turn sixty (or fifty if you are disabled). As is the case with a widower, if you are caring for a deceased worker's child who is younger than sixteen or disabled, you can collect on the worker's benefits at any age. You would not be eligible for these benefits if your own work record makes you eligible for greater benefits. If you remarry before you turn sixty (fifty if you are disabled), you will forfeit those benefits. If you remarry after age sixty, you might be able to receive the higher of the benefits payable based on either the prior or current spouse's work record. If that second marriage ends as a result of death, divorce, or annulment in less than ten years, you will again be eligible to collect benefits on your first spouse's record.

If your ex-spouse reaches retirement age and you were married for ten years and now have been divorced for more than two years, you can collect Social Security benefits at age sixty-two. Your benefits must not be greater than those of your former spouse in order for you to claim them. These benefits will terminate if you remarry.

Note, too, that if you were the working spouse during your first marriage and your ex is collecting benefits based on your earnings, your remarriage does not reduce the Social Security benefits paid to either your new spouse or your ex-spouse.

Child Receiving Social Security

If a child is under the age of eighteen or disabled, the retirement or death of a parent triggers Social Security benefits for the child. If the child is sixteen or younger, the benefit is paid to the caregiver parent. The remarriage of the surviving parent does not eliminate the benefit that the child receives. The child's benefits normally terminate at age eighteen, but they continue through to two years after graduation if the child is age eighteen or nineteen but in elementary or secondary school full-time. (If the child marries, he is no longer eligible for the benefit.) A severely disabled child whose disability began before age twenty-two is entitled to receive a parent's Social Security when that parent starts taking Social Security retirement or disability benefits, or dies. These benefits are payable beyond age eighteen until the disability ends or until the child gets married (although marrying another disabled person continues the benefit). The benefits also could decrease or be eliminated if the child becomes eligible for greater benefits on his own.

If seeking survivor benefits for a stepchild who has not been formally adopted by the stepparent, the child's parent and the number holder must have been married for one year if the number holder is alive, or for nine months if the number holder has passed away.

Robert and Scott's Story
• • • • • • • • • • • •

Scott has always wanted to have kids but feared that being gay meant fatherhood would never be a realistic option. Then he meets Robert, who has the same dream of being a parent, and also a healthy bank account to help finance the endeavor. Because they are in their late forties, they feel they ought to proceed quickly, without marrying first. They look at both adoption and surrogacy, but they live in a state that allows only married couples to adopt jointly or to do surrogacy jointly.

They choose to go through a private adoption agency, and because Robert has the greater assets and will look better to the agency, they decide that he should apply to be the initial adoptive parent. Should they be matched with a child, they think, Scott can eventually do a second-parent adoption. Robert is approved by the agency, and he adopts a daughter, Olivia. At the same time, they are fortunate enough to conceive a child through surrogacy, using Scott's sperm. The surrogate gives birth to a son that Robert and Scott name Sebastian. Here, too, they think that later Robert can do a second-parent adoption for their son.

With two infants, Robert and Scott have their hands full, and they decide to wait a few years to tie the knot, thinking that it would be nice to have Olivia be the ring bearer and Sebastian be the flower boy. They also never get around to doing the second-parent adoptions. This means that Olivia has only one legal parent, Robert, and that Sebastian has only one legal parent, Scott.

When Robert unexpectedly dies in a car accident, Scott discovers that he has serious legal problems. Even though he has been caring for Olivia ever since she was adopted, Scott has no automatic parental rights to her, as they never completed his second-parent adoption of her. Also, Scott does not get any of Robert's Social Security survivor benefits, since he is technically not a surviving spouse, and Sebastian does not get any benefits as a legal surviving child of Robert's, since they never completed Robert's second-parent adoption of him. Scott must fight Robert's family both for custody and to be the caregiver eligible for Olivia's survivor benefits as Robert's sole heir.

Governmental Benefits and Marriage

JANE A. BASSETT

Elder and disability law attorney

Bassett & Associates

Ann Arbor, Michigan

For most of my twenty years of practice as an elder and disability law attorney, I have fielded questions about marriage and divorce from a perspective of how marriage affects decision-making authority and how it affects various benefits that may be available to help cover the costs associated with aging and disability. I have railed against "family consent" laws that would allow the legal next of kin to make medical decisions for an incapacitated individual despite the presence of her life partner. I have counseled clients on how Supplemental Security Income (SSI) is affected by getting married or staying single. And I have done countless analyses of how getting married, staying married, or divorcing will affect eligibility for various Medicaid programs. With a few individual exceptions, and with the exception of SSI, being married has consistently yielded the best protections for people who need to rely on these programs.

In addition to assistance programs, legal spouses are given preference and protections throughout probate and estate matters. A legal spouse will be given preference when the court is faced with appointing a guardian or conservator for a person who becomes incapacitated. It means the difference between receiving preferential treatment and being shut out of the proceedings if the partner or spouse dies. In Michigan, the next of kin determines the disposition of a person's body when he dies. If a spouse or partner is not legally recognized, he has no authority to direct or stop a cremation, plan a funeral, or determine where the person is to be buried. In this area of the law, being legally married means the difference between being a nobody—a legal stranger—and being a person whom the law recognizes as having experienced a loss of support and partnership and who is entitled to legal protections when a spouse is ill or dies.

Marriage, however, often stands in the way of receiving assistance when a person is disabled, has minimal assets, and is not living in a nursing home. Medicaid (when a nursing home is not involved) and SSI are needs-based programs, and the regulations are very complex. In general, the married applicant's *household* has to have less than $3,000 in assets, excluding certain things such as the residence and one car. A single person can have up to $2,000 in assets. For income, a single person can have up to $450 in monthly income before completely losing the benefit for the month. However, if a person is married, the spouse's income will also be used to offset the benefit, and the benefit will be lost much sooner. Further, housing costs that are paid by someone else are deemed to be income to the applicant, and so they reduce the benefit. On the other hand, if the couple is not married and if there is a lease between them obligating the disabled partner to pay rent, the full benefit can usually be realized. While $733 a month (the 2016 SSI payment rate) does not seem like a great deal of money, for some it makes a big difference, and it has the added value of providing automatic eligibility for other programs, such as Medicaid.

Medicaid (when a nursing home is not involved) varies from state to state, but usually the couple has to have under $3,000 in countable assets in order to qualify, while an individual has to have less than $2,000. If a married couple divorces, the property division and alimony payments can sometimes be arranged to qualify the disabled spouse for assistance. Various planning tools are used, including special-needs trusts, front-loading distribution of property to the healthier spouse and then offsetting with a stream of income to the disabled spouse, and a careful analysis of which type of assets go to which spouse based on how they will be characterized in the eligibility process. A divorce attorney whose client has a disability should bring an experienced elder and disability law attorney onto the team so as not to miss an opportunity to put the client in a better position after the divorce. The goal is not to leave the disabled spouse with nothing, but rather to arrange the private resources in such a way as to allow them to be supplemented by the governmental assistance and to tap into the infrastructure of providers and suppliers that support the needs of Medicaid recipients.

I will continue to analyze whether getting married or staying married will have an impact on the benefits a person may receive when she needs care, but the difference will be that the gender of the couple should no longer have any impact. Married is married, period.

SSI AND SSDI

SSI and SSDI are two types of disability programs run by the Social Security Administration. Both require the same medical eligibility (which includes your not being able to do your job or adjust to another job because of a condition that is expected to last more than a year or result in death), but the first one places limits on the financial

HOW MARRIAGE AND PARENTAL RECOGNITION AFFECT SOCIAL SECURITY BENEFITS

Mimi and Rhonda are over 65 and collect Social Security. Mimi's benefit is $2,736/month. Rhonda's is $1,108/month. If they married, Rhonda could opt to collect half of Mimi's benefit in place of her own.

Joint household income	Monthly	Annual
Married	$4,104	$49,248
Unmarried	$3,844	$46,128
Difference	$260	$3,120

If Mimi and Rhonda were married, and Mimi were to pass away first, Rhonda could opt to collect Mimi's benefit instead of her own. The household income would be reduced by only 33% instead of 71%.

If Rhonda outlives Mimi	Monthly	Annual
Married	$2,736	$32,832
Unmarried	$1,108	$13,296
Difference	$1,628	$19,536

Thom and Antoine (both 40) are raising Antoine's daughter, Rachel. Thom passes away, having earned a benefit of $1,638. Survivor's benefits depend on whether Thom adopted Rachel and married Antoine.

Thom adopted and married	Monthly	Annual
Antoine's caregiver benefit	$1,509	$18,108
Rachel's child benefit	$1,509	$18,108
Total benefits earned	$3,108	$36,216

Thom adopted but unwed	Monthly	Annual
Antoine's caregiver benefit	$0	$0
Rachel's child benefit	$1,509	$18,108
Total benefits earned	$1,509	$18,108

Thom didn't adopt Rachel	Monthly	Annual
Antoine's caregiver benefit	$0	$0
Rachel's child benefit	$0	$0
Total benefits earned	$0	$0

resources you can have available, while the second one is available to anyone medically qualified who has a work record of paying into the system.

Supplemental Security Income (SSI) is a needs-based form of government assistance for individuals who are disabled, blind, or over age sixty-five. For SSI eligibility, individuals must prove both medical need and limited income and assets (as of this writing, an individual cannot have a monthly income of more than $733 and total assets cannot exceed $2,000). Those limits are known as the Federal Benefit Rate (FBR). Married couples receive roughly one-quarter less in SSI benefits than they would receive as two individuals living together.

Marriage results in a review of the assets and income of the spouse, as the assumption is that at least some of his resources are available for spousal support. This process is called "deeming." Instead of being double the FBR for an individual, the FBR for married couples, as of this writing, cannot exceed income of $1,100 per month and a total of $3,000 in assets. Assets from the new marital partner could reduce benefits for the eligible spouse or eliminate them altogether; be sure to check what the current FBR rate is if you are on SSI. Ask a claims representative from the Social Security Administration to help you run the numbers to be sure that marriage will not jeopardize benefits that you are relying on to survive. Also note that in some cases the Social Security Administration has sought overpayments back from married SSI recipients who previously received a benefit because both spouses' incomes were not counted when their marriages were not recognized. The calculations can be confusing because there are some things that count as income that you might not expect, and there are exemptions as well. Get assistance to make these determinations.

Supplemental Security Disability Income (SSDI) is funded by the FICA deductions in your paychecks. Once you contribute enough into the system and you are medically eligible, you can receive SSDI. Individuals can also be eligible based on the contributions of their parents or spouse during their employment histories. If you are receiving SSDI benefits based on your own work record, marriage does not affect them. SSDI benefits are not means-tested, and so eligibility does not involve an evaluation of available resources.

However, if you are receiving SSDI benefits based on the work record of a parent, those benefits end if you remarry. If you receive SSDI based on the employment record of a prior spouse from whom you are divorced, those benefits end if you remarry. And if you receive SSDI based on the eligibility of a deceased ex-spouse and you remarry before age sixty (age fifty if disabled), you will lose those surviving-spouse SSDI benefits.

The waters may be muddied in some cases if someone has been collecting Social Security based on a prior spouse's work record while in an unrecognized same-sex marriage. The question might arise as to when a marriage to someone of the same sex formally became recognized by the SSA and whether that triggers retroactive evaluation of benefits paid or due. You could have to pay back benefits based on the retroactivity of marriage recognition. For example, you could have been married to a person of the same gender for several years in an unrecognized marriage, all the while collecting benefits from your ex-spouse based on a prior hetero marriage. Investigate your rights with a capable professional, such as a lawyer who specializes in Social Security appeals. Social Security benefits are incredibly complicated.

Medicare

Medicare is a health insurance benefit for people over sixty-five years old and for people with certain disabilities. Individuals should sign up as soon as they are eligible (not waiting for the eligibility of spouses) to promptly receive the benefits. Open enrollment for Medicare is from October 15 to December 7 annually. Individuals should enroll at least three months before their sixty-fifth birthday or face penalties for failing to do so. Getting married does not affect your Medicare eligibility, as your entitlement is based on age or if you have received disability payments from Social Security for two years.

There are four parts to Medicare. Medicare Part A is hospital coverage. Part A has no premiums for most people who have worked (or who have a spouse who has worked) for at least a decade (forty quarters). Part A can also provide coverage for home health care, nursing homes, and hospice. Marriage does not have any impact on Part A because it is free. However, if you have not worked long enough to be eligible on your own, marriage to someone eligible entitles you to Part A coverage.

Medicare Part B is medical coverage for doctor visits, lab results, and some other outpatient medical services. Part B does require payment of a monthly premium, which is based on the collective annual income of you and your spouse. Marriage will impact your Part B premium in that the coverage will be more costly the more you and your spouse earn together.

Parts A and B are collectively known as "original Medicare," and those are the benefits you get automatically once you start collecting Social Security. Original Medicare is provided directly by the government. Conversely, Parts C and D are provided by private companies who contract with the federal government.

Part C is the Medicare Advantage Plan. Part C is not a separate benefit, but rather is the option for a private insurance company to provide the services of Medicare Parts A and B through a plan such as an HMO or PPO. Part D, the prescription drug benefit, requires an additional premium.

Parts C and D are individual plans; marriage has no impact. Even if you and your spouse sign up for identical plans, each of you will have separate premiums, copays, and deductibles. Likewise with the many Part D options—choosing the same plan will not bring any cost savings for you and your spouse, as each of you must satisfy individual deductibles before Medicare kicks in and provides coverage.

Medicare is not a means-tested benefit. Individuals are eligible for the benefit without regard to income. Coverage does not change based on marital status. If you have enough work credits to be eligible for Social Security, or your spouse or former spouse does, then you are eligible for Medicare. Premiums are determined by several factors, including work history, income, and resources. Marriage impacts the premiums for certain benefits because a spouse's income and resources are included in the calculations.

Medicare does not provide more than one hundred days in a rehabilitation facility after discharge from a hospital. If you need additional assistance with activities of daily living such as dressing, bathing, toileting, and feeding and you do not have supplemental insurance or savings to cover it, Medicaid is the program that covers these expenses.

Medicaid

Medicaid is a state-run program with some federal funds that provides health and long-term care insurance coverage for lower-income people. Eligibility is based on household income and assets. Marriage can change eligibility for benefits. Issues around Medicaid are thorny and complex. All individuals receiving Medicaid should examine their situation carefully prior to marrying.

Back in the mid-2000s, as marriage equality started its march forward, I speculated that while our intention was for marriage to be a shield to protect us, it would likely be used first as a sword to harm us. It was an awfully cynical thought, but it did not take long for a prime example to present itself. A couple who were legally married in Massachusetts but whose marriage was not recognized in their home state of Florida reached out to me. One was a long-term HIV survivor getting life-prolonging medications through Medicaid. He was contacted with an inquiry about his household income. He did not want to have to report the income of his spouse for fear that he would lose the Medicaid benefits that allowed him access to his treatment. Paradoxically, this couple had to argue for the *invalidity* of their marriage to continue life-saving medical care.

If one spouse needs to go into a long-term care facility or have long-term care provided at home and you do not have sufficient insurance to cover it, Medicaid will step in if you are eligible based on assets and income. Medicaid is available only if you have assets that do not exceed a certain amount; the eligibility amounts change annually. There are spousal impoverishment protections for married couples, so that the spouse not entering a facility is able to keep more of her assets and does not need to "spend down" enough to make her spouse eligible to enter the home. These protections for the spouse living in the community, not in a facility (known as the "community spouse," which is not to be confused with a spouse in a community property state), can be essential to ensuring that the community spouse is able to age with dignity and independence. This is an important benefit of marriage. Medicaid is very diligent at ascertaining whether the household income and assets are too high for qualification. Take great care in deciding to marry if either of you are taking advantage of these benefits or expect to do so.

"Spousal refusal" is where the healthy spouse has assets in excess of the amount allowed by the spousal impoverishment protections and alleges that she will not support the medically needy spouse. A few states have a provision for spousal refusal when a spouse is getting home care. When receiving nursing home care, all married spouses can avail themselves of this benefit; it is a federal right. When spousal refusal is invoked, the well spouse is able to retain assets in excess of what is called the "community spouse resource allowance" (at this point hovering around $120,000). Medicaid should not and cannot look at her income or assets for support and instead must itself provide coverage to the needy spouse. It sounds harsh, but spousal refusal can be an important vehicle to protect remaining assets for your own care as you age.

An elder care lawyer can help with this to be sure you handle the planning properly. This is a particularly tricky area of the law because it is ever-changing and varies greatly by state. Work with someone who has a deep knowledge of how to navigate these issues. See the resources section at the end of this book for how to find lawyer members of the National Association of Elder Law Attorneys (NAELA), who specialize in elder care law.

OTHER GOVERNMENTAL BENEFITS: SNAP, TANF, WIC, AND HOUSING SUBSIDIES

The Supplemental Nutrition Assistance Program (SNAP) is a federal program administered by the U.S. Department of Agriculture to help lower-income people afford groceries. The food assistance provided is based on household size and income. If married, a couple will be considered part of the same household. Marriage will result in the income of both spouses being calculated for eligibility. The practical effect of marriage is exclusion from SNAP eligibility; often only unmarried people are able to obtain this benefit.

Temporary Assistance for Needy Families (TANF) is a limited benefit designed to give small amounts of money and child care on a short-term basis to families in dire straits. Individual states run TANF with federal funds; the amount of funds and duration available vary by state. To receive funds, individuals must participate in a welfare-to-work program. Marriage to someone with an income raises household income, often beyond the qualifying level for TANF. Even if the family is still eligible, marriage can subject another person to what is known as the welfare-to-work requirement and possibly limit access to child care benefits. However, if both partners are legal parents, marriage will likely not effect eligibility, since you are already considered one household for eligibility purposes if you cohabitate. Each state and circumstance is different. Consult an attorney in your state if this is a concern for you.

Women, Infants, and Children (WIC) is a special supplemental nutrition program for pregnant women and kids. Eligibility is based on household income. To be eligible, a woman must be pregnant or have just given birth. Infants up to a year old and children up to five years old are also eligible. In addition, there is a nutritional risk requirement, and screening for this is done at WIC clinics nationwide. Typically, if one is financially eligible for SNAP or Medicaid, one is also eligible for WIC. Household income is one of the criteria for eligibility; the higher the total income, the more likely you would not be eligible for the program.

If you are receiving housing assistance or a housing subsidy (which can be from any combination of federal, state, county, and municipal sources), check the income and asset limits for qualifying. Eligibility could be jeopardized if you marry, increasing your household income and assets. Speaking of housing, while new rules are better than ever before, LGBT people have relatively few protections against housing discrimination at the national and local levels. Marrying could result in a perfectly legal eviction. Stories abound of landlords around the country claiming that their tenants' marriage offends their religious beliefs and kicking them out. Without housing protections, some newlyweds become homeless with no legal recourse.

Lest we focus only on the financial impact of marriage, however, William Singer reminds us not to lose sight of the emotional significance of marriage in this cameo.

"More Secure and Freer"

WILLIAM SINGER

Founder, LGBT Family Law Institute

Singer & Fedun

Belle Mead, New Jersey

With the advent of marriage equality, attorneys and accountants who represent lesbian, gay, and bisexual clients are asked to analyze whether marriage makes sense for their clients. Many of these clients, in decades-long relationships, question the need for a "piece of paper" to prove their commitment.

Others want to undertake a financial calculation—weighing issues such as the income tax marriage penalty, the tax advantages for a surviving spouse who inherits a retirement account, and Social Security benefits, among others.

For clients who receive means-tested benefits or who are facing a costly debilitating illness, marriage is not an option when it could compromise benefits or put a well partner's assets at risk. For most, however, there are economic pros and cons with no clear-cut answer.

I counsel clients to add to their monetary calculation the intangible societal and emotional consequences of being married. Let's get real—marriage is a status widely recognized, honored, and respected in our society and throughout the world. The status has incalculable value.

It is interesting that so many of those clients who questioned whether marriage was for them have come back to report that getting married had an unexpected, deep emotional impact. As one exuberant sixty-five-year-old newlywed recounted, "I feel both more secure and freer."

MILITARY SERVICE

Military benefits are a major asset both for those who are on active or reserve duty and for those who have served in the past. There are a variety of military benefits, and they can seem confusing to navigate, but the rewards for figuring them out are substantial. Roughly a third of the total compensation received for one's military service is paid as base pay; the remaining two-thirds is paid in the form of in-kind benefits such as housing, subsistence allowances, clothing and travel allowances, medical and dental care, and much more. Upon marriage, many of those benefits are increased on the presumption that the needs of two are greater than the needs of one. There are a host of programs that help a military spouse with access to education and employment as well as provide excellent medical, dental, vision, and mental health care through the Tricare plan available to service members.

Other military benefits that accrue to a spouse include child care, burial rights with the military member at national cemeteries, military identification cards, travel on military aircraft when available, joint duty assignments, and disability and death compensation. Many military benefits end at the service member's death unless the service member enrolls in a Survivor Benefit Plan (SBP), which provides an annuity to the surviving spouse through which she can continue to receive benefits.

In order to enroll a spouse for military benefits, the member of the military needs to go in person to an ID office or a Defense Enrollment Eligibility Reporting System (DEERS) office within a month of the marriage with a copy of the marriage license or certificate. If you were married and then the marriage later became recognized in your home state, just head over to inform the military of the marriage as soon as possible.

Spouses of LGBT service members might not be able to travel together to an overseas tour. Laws must be favorable to LGBT persons in that host nation, and there are not many such nations, especially in the regions where our military is stationed. Before sending you to a location outside the United States, the Department of Defense and Department of State must determine that there will be no issue there with the recognition of your union. The government says that this measure is necessary to ensure that appropriate legal protections are in place for service members and their spouses.

Veterans' spouses can take advantage of a host of benefits that can truly make life easier, especially during life's tougher times. Service members can be eligible for these Department of Veterans Affairs (VA) benefits based upon criteria including the nature of discharge, the completion of a certain period of time in active service with the proper type of discharge or retirement after twenty years in service, or certain types of injuries sustained during service.

Prior to the 2010 repeal of the law that made the "don't ask, don't tell" policy necessary, some 114,000 gay and lesbian service members were discharged under less than fully honorable conditions because of their sexual orientation. Such a discharge classification prevents them from accessing VA benefits. There have been legislative efforts to revisit these classifications, but none have been successful. A few advocates have been able to assist service members with changes to their discharge documents. In addition to opening doors to service members, success in reclassifying discharges would provide countless same-sex spouses with spousal veteran benefits they also deserve.

An example of how discrimination that occurred prior to the elimination of the "don't ask, don't tell" policy continues to harm real people is the Montgomery GI Bill. The GI Bill is for education including college or vocational trainings. One of the criteria for GI Bill eligibility is an honorable discharge. For the spouse of a post-9/11 service member who is otherwise eligible for the GI Bill, there is a spousal GI Bill that would cover her education as well. The ripple effect of a less than honorable discharge can be a real game changer for some families.

There are benefits available to the spouse of a veteran who becomes disabled or dies either in active service or as a result of a service-connected disability. Aid and Assistance is a great VA benefit for couples. It is a tax-free allowance available to veterans and spouses over age sixty-five to offset the costs of long-term nursing care needs, either in the home or at a facility. Individuals providing in-home care for a veteran who served after 9/11 and was injured in the line of duty can receive benefits including counseling, training, and support. If serving as the veteran's primary caregiver, you might be entitled to both a monthly stipend and the providing of a free caregiver for thirty days annually in order to take time off from those taxing duties. A particularly nice feature of this program is that you need not be legally married to the veteran. As long as you live together and meet the other criteria, you should be eligible for these caregiver benefits.

Another great benefit is the VA Guaranteed Home Loan Program. In this program, the government guarantees a mortgage for the service member to purchase a home without the usual required down payment. A spouse can utilize this benefit if she is the surviving spouse of a veteran who died either on active duty or because of a disability that resulted from her military service. Also, the surviving spouse of any veteran who had a previous VA loan may refinance that loan through the program.

Military Benefits

BRIDGET J. WILSON

Civilian military attorney and consulting counsel for Service Members, Partners, Allies for Respect and Tolerance for All

San Diego, California

An avalanche of change has tumbled down on LGBT service members since December 2010. They have seen the repeal of the statute that created the policy often called "don't ask, don't tell." That repeal went into effect nearly a year later, in September 2011. The battles for marriage equality took them to *United States v. Windsor* in 2013, which compelled federal recognition of marriages between persons of the same sex. And in 2015, after *Obergefell*, marriage was declared a fundamental right for same-sex couples nationwide.

After *Windsor*, the services began to recognize the marriages of these service members and made most of the benefits of service available to their spouses. But the gaps in equality became very clear. Service members do not choose where they will live, and many military bases are located in states that refused to recognize their marriages or enforced specific statutory and state constitutional prohibitions on their marriages. In spite of the decision in *Obergefell*, service members likely will confront continuing difficulties in the states that are resisting recognition of their marriages.

In addition, the situation for transgender service members remains tenuous. The repeal of "don't ask, don't tell" did not change regulations barring the service of known trans persons, although there has been progress, with some service-specific changes determining that there is no medical basis for the automatic separation of trans service members. That battle continues.

Married LGBT persons must continue to be prepared for difficulties with local authorities. The random emergency room clerk, the apartment complex manager, or the county clerk may resist an individual's assertion that she is a military spouse not only out of bigotry but also out of lack of knowledge. Paper pushers with malicious intent or simple confusion can make the life of the service member and spouse more difficult than it should be. It is also possible that they will be confronted with an obstructionist individual within the military. For that reason, many of the following suggested protective measures are identical to the pre-*Obergefell* advice:

1. Obtain several official copies of the marriage certificate. An obstructionist bureaucrat will find it easy to reject a photocopy when you are seeking to qualify for benefits. That is also true for any other official documents that the service member may be required to present to qualify for benefits and services. A military dependent's birth certificate is an example.

2. Be aware that a number of states will deny access to state benefits offered to military spouses of the opposite sex in their efforts to continue opposition to marriage equality. For example, many states offer reduced tuition or in-state tuition rates to military spouses. Officials opposing marriage

equality may reject same-sex spouses seeking the benefits otherwise offered to military dependents. This is work that will keep advocacy groups busy for the foreseeable future.

3. Take advantage of the military's Legal Services Offices (LSO). If possible, service members should consider comprehensive family legal planning with attorneys who have expertise in dealing with same-sex couples. There are many LSOs whose attorneys are excellent providers of these services. The LSOs may be limited in what they can offer—for example, many cannot offer certain kinds of trusts even if it would be wise for the service member and spouse to have a trust. Sometimes civilian attorneys are unaware of the special needs of service members. Service members and their spouses still need to educate themselves and ask many questions.

4. Service members need to ensure that they have changed or executed the documents that protect family members. In most circumstances a legally recognized spouse will be the person entitled to obtain the service member's death benefits. But some benefits, such as the Service Members Group Life Insurance (SGLI), passes to the person who is listed as the beneficiary. Often service members join at a young age and list a parent as the beneficiary of their SGLI. If the service member fails to change the beneficiary after marriage, the parent will receive the benefit in the event of the service member's death. It is important to update personnel records.

5. The state courts are another challenge. Because divorce, separation, division of property, child custody, and adoptions are within the jurisdiction of the state courts, those are expected to be the next battleground for marriage equality. Service members are often a captive population in hostile states; it is likely that these service members will face problems with family law matters and will need to seek the assistance of knowledgeable civilian attorneys. As a general rule, with few exceptions, military attorneys cannot go into the civilian courts on behalf of a service member and his family.

As was true of marriage equality before *Windsor*, service members have often been treated in ways that are examples of inequality in action. It created a stir when commanders found their soldiers struggling to take care of the simplest of family readiness tasks. Such inequalities immediately impact this most uniform of institutions. There are challenges within the institution—one example is the refusal of some military chaplains to perform or provide services for LGBT service members, fed by the misleading "religious freedom" movement against marriage equality. Still, the rapid societal progress is reflected in changes in the services. Recently the Department of Defense announced that it would include sexual orientation in the Equal Opportunity program, a move that makes it possible for service members to raise complaints of harassment and discrimination based on sexual orientation that were not available to them before that change.

Following the decision in *Obergefell*, the Department of Veterans Affairs announced that it would provide spousal benefits for the spouses of veterans and deceased veterans. The VA had been denying spousal benefits to those in same-sex marriages who resided in states that did not recognize the marriages.

The agency had issued this statement:

For the purpose of VA benefits, spousal status is predicated on a valid marriage under state law. Under the current Federal law, 38 U.S.C. § 103(c), VA may recognize a Veteran's marriage for VA purposes if:

- the marriage was legal in the place where the Veteran or the Veteran's spouse lived at the time of the marriage; or
- the marriage was legal in the place where the Veteran or the Veteran's spouse lived when he or she filed a VA claim or application (or a later date when the Veteran became eligible for benefits).

Some VA regional offices denied benefits for all same-sex spouses based on a statute that defined marriage as between a man and woman. Presumably that has changed, as the VA has issued a news release indicating that VA offices "may" grant benefits and that the agency will be issuing formal guidance later.

Any veteran refused benefits or told that she is ineligible for spousal benefits should request that determination in writing with the reasoning for that decision and appeal the finding.

There remain challenges that service members are uniquely positioned to address. A simple example is businesses that refuse to do business with LGBT service members and their families. With the assistance of support groups, service members can take this problem to their commands. The services expect that local businesses will treat all service members with respect and assist them equally. When they do not, they risk being declared "off-limits," with all service members prohibited from patronizing the business. We saw this in 2014, when an Air Force command declared off-limits some Oklahoma City area restaurants whose owner openly discriminates against African Americans and LGBT people. That kind of leverage is unique to the military environment, which for all its flaws is officially protective of its members.

For LGBT service members, the preventative advice has not changed: Be prepared and document your relationship. Be certain to line up resources for any challenges you face. Be proactive in protecting yourself as we move forward. We are already seeing a number of service members who have never served in an LGB-exclusive military. The road to trans equality in the military is before us, using the example of our allies in Britain, Canada, and Australia. There are many remaining challenges, but no group is better prepared to tackle those challenges than service members and their families.

IMMIGRATION

When someone from another country wants to live and work in the United States legally, immigration is the path to follow. As a lawyer based in the multicultural city of Miami, I see many people who have suffered from the harmful effects of our country's immigration policies. A great benefit of recent changes in U.S. law is that binational same-sex couples can now marry and secure citizenship for the nonresident member of the couple.

United States Customs and Immigration Services (USCIS), an agency of the federal government, decides who can stay within U.S. borders. USCIS policy allows a citizen spouse married to someone who is not a U.S. citizen to sponsor her spouse for immigration benefits and have her status changed. This adjustment of status is colloquially called "getting a green card." If the couple is not yet married but seeks to be, they can obtain a fiancé(e) visa and then marry within ninety days of the fiancé(e)'s arrival in the United States.

Bruce and Miguel's Story

•••••••••••••

We've met Bruce and Miguel earlier in this chapter, when we were discussing the tax implications of marriage. But before they married, Miguel and Bruce were together for five years. Bruce is a U.S. citizen, and Miguel was here on a tourist visa from his native country in South America. Miguel had been going back and forth between his country and the United States using tourist visas, but both Bruce and Miguel wanted Miguel to remain in the United States permanently. One solution to this immigration drama was for Bruce and Miguel to formalize their relationship through marriage. Marriage meant that Bruce could sponsor Miguel for immigration benefits so that Miguel could become a permanent resident, then eventually obtain citizenship.

As Bruce and Miguel learned, however, getting married wasn't that simple. Tourist visas are valid only for a limited time, and, just as with student visas, there can be no "intent to remain" in the United States. Their immigration lawyer explained that they had to be careful, because marriage is considered evidence of intent to remain in the United States, and Miguel could face an allegation of visa fraud. The lawyer suggested that Miguel go back home one last time, then apply for a fiancé visa to bring him back to the United States. They got the fiancé visa, Miguel came back to the United States, and Bruce and Miguel married within the required three months of Miguel's arrival in the country. The immigration lawyer then submitted the paperwork to USCIS to secure a green card for Miguel. When Bruce and Miguel went for their interview, the USCIS officer asked lots of personal questions, such as what kind of toothpaste the other uses, and reviewed photos of their travels together. Bruce and Miguel had to prove that they were emotionally and financially a committed couple. Fortunately, they passed, the application was approved within a few months, and Miguel got a green card.

Recent changes in the law benefit same-sex binational couples enormously, but there are some cautions. USCIS scrutinizes all marriages carefully. Any marriage entered into for immigration purposes and not for love and commitment is determined a sham. According to some immigration attorneys who have been working with same-sex couples since this spousal sponsorship benefit became available, some USCIS agents scrutinize same-sex couples more closely, singling out LGBT couples for more difficult and even inappropriate questions. If USCIS agents determine that a marriage is a sham, the government brings a felony charge against the citizen spouse and deports the noncitizen. The noncitizen spouse cannot reenter the United States for at least a decade. Furthermore, the noncitizen spouse can never again present a marriage to USCIS for immigration benefit. Still, for loving binational couples like Bruce and Miguel, this legal development can be a real life (and relationship) saver.

USCIS's stated policy is that same-sex marriages are to be treated exactly the same as different-sex marriages. In reality, that is not always the case. When navigating the immigration process, it is important to be represented by a knowledgeable immigration attorney who is comfortable working with the LGBT community. If you go it alone, immigration officers are more apt to give you a hard time; they tend to behave themselves when there is a lawyer present to hold them accountable. In addition, while the forms involved in the immigration process might seem quite easy, there are many nuances in the application process, especially for same-sex couples.

MOMS AND MOMS, DADS AND DADS

Marriage affects parents in significant ways. Inform yourself about your state's law if you have children, or plan to have them. Family law differs dramatically from state to state. Familiarize yourself with the particular laws of your state. Here is a brief overview of some issues around marriage and parenting.

Child Support

Whether you are paying or receiving child support, marrying again should not affect the amount paid. Child support is the *child's* money, not the parent's money, and it is based on the earnings of the biological or legal parents. This can change, however, if your new spouse's income significantly reduces your obligation to pay for certain household items, or you voluntarily reduce or terminate your own income due to your spouse's income and then try to point to your individual financial circumstances as a basis to reduce your support obligations or increase the support you are receiving. The parent paying child support can argue that less support should be paid when the new spouse's household contributions mean that more funds are now available to support the child or children. Before remarrying, check with the lawyer who helped you negotiate the terms of your divorce to be clear about what impact remarrying will have on the deal you struck. You might be jeopardizing spousal or child support that has been awarded to you; be careful. (If you are receiving alimony from a former spouse and considering cohabitating, entering into a supportive relationship, or marrying again, please see "Alimony from a Prior Marriage" in this chapter and Chapter 10, "Nuptial Agreements," for more information.)

Parental Rights to a Nonbiological Child

If I had a dollar for every person who explained that one of the reasons she wants to marry her partner was to have automatic parental rights, I would be one ridiculously wealthy woman. Unfortunately, parental rights are not that simple. The irrefutable path to parental rights is to secure a parentage or adoption judgment. A court order that clearly and unequivocally states who a child's parents are will be enforceable anywhere because of the doctrine of "full faith and credit"—the United States Constitution requires that all states respect the judicial proceedings of every other state. That means that if you have a judgment conferring parental rights upon you in one place and then you suffer a breakup, your ex cannot decamp with the child to another less friendly jurisdiction and claim that you have no parental rights there. The other critical legal term here is "marital presumption of parentage." Marital presumption, also known as the presumption of legitimacy, means that married individuals are assumed to be the parents of a child born into their marriage. Sounds great, right? I mean, your partner gives birth to a kid and you are married to her, so the kid is yours too now, no matter what, right? Not necessarily. Marital presumption is rebuttable in some states, meaning spouses can challenge the presumption and win. Some judges have already found that marital presumption cannot apply to a same-sex couple, although challenges to these rules are ongoing. Some of the worst cases for gay parents around the country have occurred in the context of a breakup where judges give the benefit of the doubt to the biological parent, who alleges that the other parent is unfit, claims that the other parent did not want the child to begin with, or makes some other argument that the marital presumption is not appropriate and should not be applied. A few recent cases involved appellate courts finding that a marital presumption could not possibly apply to the partner of a biological mom because the presumption is meant to protect biological fathers, not nonbiological mothers, although other cases have properly applied the presumption to same-sex spouses. Regardless of whether we are biological parents to our children, we do want courts to construe the marital presumption to apply to us. Parentage or adoption judgments are the only legal remedies to prevent the loss of parental rights. Some states do strongly protect nonbiological parents who were married at the time their children were born, but many states have not yet addressed this question or do not strongly protect these parents. For this reason, an adoption or a parentage judgment is needed, even if you live in a friendly state, to protect your parental rights no matter where you move or travel.

The way to avoid contentious court battles over parental rights is for the nonbiological parent to secure a court order affirming parental rights. This court order remains as important as ever. Marriage does not change the need for it. A judgment is respected everywhere in the world. It is a drag to have to still adopt a child you have been raising, even if you are on the birth certificate. Being on the birth certificate is an important start but you—and your child—deserve more. It is frustrating that marriage does not ensure the full legal protections of all loving moms and dads. For the time being, though, protect yourself and your family.

The Marital Presumption

DEBORAH WALD

Chair, National Family Law Advisory Council for the National Center for Lesbian Rights

Wald Law Group

San Francisco, California

The marital presumption is a long-standing legal assumption that when a married woman gives birth, her husband is the father of her child. It predates the ability to determine genetic paternity by DNA testing, and historically was a primary way of assigning men financial responsibility for children.

Given that it now is very easy to determine genetic paternity, the continued usefulness of the marital presumption is an issue of significant debate. As with many family law issues, different states take different positions: in some states, the marital presumption is automatically rebutted by proof of genetic nonpaternity, whereas in other states marital presumption has been taken to express a public policy that marital families should be protected, and the presumption therefore survives evidence that the husband is not the genetic father.

Application of the marital presumption to married lesbian couples will vary from state to state, largely depending on the state's application of the marital presumption to husbands who are not the genetic fathers of the children to whom their wives give birth. As a matter of equal protection, a state should not be able to deny marital protection to the wife of a woman giving birth if the state would protect the husband of a woman giving birth under similar circumstances. But this is not always the case.

For example, in California, we have two separate marital presumptions: the "conclusive" marital presumption and the "rebuttable" marital presumption. The conclusive marital presumption strictly speaking applies only where the child is conceived during the marriage and the husband is neither impotent nor sterile. In other words, for application of the conclusive marital presumption to be technically correct, the husband has to establish that he had both the opportunity and the physiological ability to impregnate his wife. Since a lesbian spouse does not have the physiological ability to impregnate her wife, the conclusive marital presumption generally will not be applied to lesbian couples. However, California's rebuttable marital presumption requires only that the couple be married when the child is born; thus, this presumption clearly will apply to married lesbian couples. But this rebuttable presumption provides only a legal starting place; it is open to being disproved under a variety of circumstances. It therefore is not safe to rely on as a permanent method of establishing parental rights. Application of the marital presumption to gay men having babies is far more problematic. There is no presumption that the wife of a married man who fathers a child with another woman out of wedlock is the mother of the child—the woman giving birth is commonly accepted as the mother. Therefore, if a heterosexual wife gains no legal status when another woman gives birth to her husband's child, a gay husband also is unlikely to gain any legal status when a woman gives birth to his husband's child. However, because gay men having babies generally do so through a surrogacy process, surrogacy laws may well afford them legal protections completely separate from the marital presumption. They therefore are far less likely to need to look to marital presumptions to establish parental rights than lesbian couples, who often engage in assisted insemination and give birth to children without doctors or lawyers involved.

The marital presumption provides married lesbian couples having children with the wonderful convenience of being able to get both of their names on their child's birth certificate without a court order. However, because application of the marital presumption to married lesbian couples across the country will be varied and sometimes problematic—and, importantly, because application of the marital presumption does not provide interstate protection under the "full faith and credit" clause of the U.S. Constitution—family law attorneys and the national LGBT organizations continue to strongly recommend that these couples follow up with either a confirmatory adoption (the procedure for which will vary depending on state law) or a parentage action under their state's Uniform Parentage Act or other parentage law.

Tania and Marie's Story

• • • • • • • • • • • •

Tania and Marie, whom we met earlier in the discussion of income taxes, are married and decide to have a child through assisted insemination. At first Marie is on the fence about the sacrifices they will have to make in their lives to have a child, but out of love for her wife, she participates in every step of Tania's pregnancy, including choosing the sperm donor, going to all of the birthing classes, and cutting the umbilical cord. Marie falls head over heels in love with baby Emma even before she arrives. Once the baby comes home, Marie and Tania equally co-parent and their baby thrives. Sadly, though, their relationship does not survive the stress of having a child and they have an acrimonious breakup. At the time of their separation, Tania and Marie have not done a second-parent or stepparent adoption to solidify Marie's parental rights because Marie believes that she has parental rights by virtue of their marriage—her name is on Emma's birth certificate. Tania hires a lawyer to help her prove that Marie should not have parental rights because she never wanted Emma. Marie is shocked to learn that Tania is going to do everything in her power to rebut any presumption of Marie's parental rights through an expensive and protracted custody battle. Now, whether she gets to see Emma at all is in the hands of a stranger—a judge who does not know them or their family. Tania and Marie were married before they had Emma, and the best-case scenario is that the judge that their case lands in front of finds it to be in the best interests of the child that the marital presumption applies.

Some states have specific requirements that the nonbiological parent execute a consent or some other document evidencing her intent to co-parent. Make sure you are knowledgeable about any such laws, and get it in writing if need be. The National Center for Lesbian Rights has great state-by-state resources on its website, and a toll-free helpline for more information about your state law: 800-528-6257.

If the child was born before you married, you likely would not benefit from the marital presumption, except in some states. The child technically was not born into this marriage except in states that apply the marital presumption to children born before marriage, although how these laws will apply to LGBT parents is still unclear in most states. Most of the current state laws that provide the presumption do so in laws strictly and narrowly written to apply to finding a presumption of paternity (fatherhood) for a man who has a child with a woman and later marries her.

Rather than potentially subject yourself and your children to a costly and lengthy litigation battle while your court must look to other state's legal decisions that are all over the map, you should take the affirmative step of legalizing the parental relationship. There is much misinformation circulating about parental rights. Many same-sex couples believe that by marrying they magically get unequivocal parental rights to the children their partners bore or adopted prior to their marriage. That could not be further from the truth. Marriage generally does not confer parental rights for preexisting children. Stepparent adoption is an ideal way to create and confirm parental rights in these situations.

Often, same-sex couples express upset at having to go through these "hoops," complaining that heterosexual couples do not. This perception is wrong! Different-sex couples frequently do stepparent adoptions. Sometimes it is just to be on the safe side and leave no room for doubt, and other times there are concerns that the state's law does not protect unmarried biological fathers and it is best to confer inviolable parental rights with an adoption. Stepparent adoption is not an adoption in the same way that you might adopt a child through the foster care system or privately through an adoption agency. It is a simpler process that clarifies the rights and responsibilities each parent has to the child and to each other as co-parents.

These battles can arise not just in the case of breakup but also at the incapacity or death of the biological parent. Clarity about parental rights is essential. Button it up with a judgment from a court. If you are the nonbiological parent, it has happened and remains possible that a hostile court somewhere could decide that since you could have adopted the child to ensure your parental rights but chose not to, that choice is somehow a surrender of those rights. Decisions like those are still happening with alarming frequency. Parental rights are an ever-evolving area of the law. Advocates for LGBT families hope these cautions will not be necessary forever, but at the moment it is important to be clear about parental rights and to handle them with care and an abundance of caution.

If you are married, a stepparent adoption, a less rigorous process with fewer hurdles, will secure parental rights to your spouse's biological or adopted child. Usually stepparent adoptions do not require a home study (a series of home visits and background checks done when someone wishes to adopt a child).

We colloquially call these types of adoptions, done for a child born into a marital relationship, confirmatory adoptions. It is an accurate description: confirmatory adoptions solidify parental rights presumed upon marriage. In some states where a couple's prior marriage was recognized after the child was born, a lawyer can obtain an order "legitimizing" the child (giving her two legal parents). Whatever you want to call it, that judgment is conclusive proof, which cannot be contested, that you are the parent—no ifs, ands, or buts.

If you are not married, solidifying parental rights is called second-parent adoption. Second-parent adoption often, but not in every state, involves a home study and a brief court hearing. Not every state and not every judge will allow these adoptions for unmarried parents. It is important to have the case handled by a lawyer experienced in these specific cases for the LGBT community.

There are many reasons couples might choose to remain unmarried. If they have children, both should have full and complete parental rights unconnected to their marital status. Some courts and some states think that second-parent adoptions can be phased out since any same-sex couple that has kids can marry and do a stepparent adoption. This line of thinking is scary. No one should be forced to marry to obtain or preserve parental rights.

Couples who choose not to marry are one example of people for whom it is important to preserve second-parent adoptions. Advocates also want to keep second-parent adoptions even after marriage equality in order to have a vehicle to protect the parental rights of a former partner after a breakup. This plays out when an unmarried couple who are raising a child together break up. If they did not already secure a second-parent adoption, the person who is not the legal parent is vulnerable to losing co-parenting rights of custody, decision-making, and time-sharing rights if the split is adversarial. Very often a couple might separate but still elect to co-parent and complete a second-parent adoption because they jointly recognize what is in the best interest of the child. In some states, there were bans on second-parent adoptions; these bans were later removed so that individuals could, at long last, establish parental rights with the children they were raising. If the parents had already broken up before the law changed, we would hope that they could still complete a second-parent adoption to solidify parental rights.

Whether you choose a stepparent adoption or a second-parent adoption, both parents likely will go to court for a brief hearing as part of the legal process. In court, you will testify before a judge that you both agree that this adoption is irrevocable and in the best interests of the child. A court hearing is nothing to fear. They are typically very sweet, quick exchanges after which you take a group picture with the judge and create a nice family memory of the day you became legally united. If your child is a bit older when you are going through this process and you do not want him to hear the term "adoption" for fear that he will have some negative associations or feel unsafe that his daddies were not both legally his parents, see if there is a way that you can have a friend or family member sit with him just outside the courtroom. That way, he does not hear the testimony or judge's ruling but still can have the fun part after the hearing of coming in to pose for a picture and maybe even bang a gavel. Some judges allow you to appear via telephone for the hearing. Check with your lawyer.

An adoption or parentage judgment provides a certainty that a birth certificate listing both parents does not provide. A birth certificate is evidence of who the parents are, but it is not irrebuttable proof (that is, beyond question), nor does it confer any legal parental rights. If you are in a recognized relationship such as a marriage (some states will still recognize your civil union or domestic partnership for these purposes), that status will allow both of you to be listed on the child's birth certificate. With some restrictions, you can put almost anyone you want on your child's birth certificate but again, that is presumptive, *not* conclusive, proof of parentage. Again, there is that legal term about a presumption and the potential for that presumption to be somehow disputed or set aside. The judgment ties it up in a bow, leaving no room for a successful challenge to parental rights anywhere.

With only twenty-one countries currently recognizing same-sex marriage, these situations will continue to arise with unfortunate frequency. This is yet another example of what can go wrong when relying solely on a birth certificate to establish parental rights. We see case after case after an acrimonious breakup where the initial legal parent absconds with the child to another jurisdiction that does not recognize the relationship status, putting the rights of the other parent in jeopardy. This also occurs when the initial legal parent passes away and his family or an agency of the government such as the Social Security Administration steps in and successfully argues that the birth certificate is not enough to establish parental rights without an order from a court finalizing an adoption or finding legal parentage. By contrast, a court order confirming parental rights is hard to dispute. This situation is unfortunate and unfair, but that's the way it is at the moment.

Adopting Nonbiological Children

The reason the emphasis here is on biological and not adoptive parents is that often when a child is adopted, the couple, if married, adopts together. Therefore, when a child is adopted either from foster care or privately from a birth mom with whom arrangements are made pre-birth, it is typically done as a joint adoption resulting in both parents having full legal rights to the child from birth. This has not always been possible because of restrictions in the law, and it is an issue that remains in flux in some states that are still getting used to their newfound marriage equality and bringing their adoption laws in line. Also, as we have learned, some parents will not be married for a host of reasons. They will do the initial adoption of the child and follow it up with a second-parent adoption.

The moral of the story is that you should do what you can to get the most comprehensive legal protections for the child you are raising, so that if your family encounters any of the three big D's (divorce, disability, or death), the issue of who is a legal parent does not muddy the waters. I have seen lots of clients whose parental rights were in jeopardy until their union was recognized and many more for whom that recognition came too late, after they had already lost their children. Cases involving angry exes who are biological or otherwise legal parents have made the worst law for LGBT people, in many cases far worse than those decisions that arose from custody battles after a hetero marriage dissolved.

All this assumes that you want the parental rights to begin with. If you are married to someone with a child and you are not the legal parent or interested in becoming one, the marriage itself does not create any rights or obligations. If you were to split, you are typically not required to pay child support, nor do you get time sharing.

Reflecting on those big D's is important because you are not just protecting your parental rights against the potential bad acts of the other in the event of divorce, but also against the outside world in the event of disability or death.

Robert, Scott, Sebastian, and Olivia's Story

••••••••••••••••••••••••••••••

As we saw earlier, Robert and Scott did not get around to estate planning, second-parent adoptions, or marrying before Robert died in a car accident. They just trusted that everything would work out okay, and they certainly did not anticipate the accident. Instead Robert has left behind a partner, Scott, and a son, Sebastian, both of whom are legal strangers to him. Absent proper planning, Robert has one legal heir: the daughter he adopted alone, Olivia.

Without a document signed by Robert giving Scott the power to make medical and educational decisions for Olivia, Scott faces challenges when taking her to the doctor or dealing with her school. If Robert had done a designation of guardian in the event of his disability or death, Scott could have gone to court to at least be appointed Olivia's legal guardian. Because Scott is not legally recognized, however, he needs to fight Robert's family for parental rights to Olivia, whom the family only wants custody of because of the funds that come along with her through Robert's estate.

Side note: In the story above, Scott was the only legal parent of their son, Sebastian, because of restrictions in their state's surrogacy law. Surrogacy laws are very state-specific and are presently in flux. If you want to know about the laws in your state and the role marriage and genetic connections play in the legal process, Creative Family Connections has a great state-by-state guide to surrogacy laws on its website at surrogacymap.com.

HOSPITAL VISITATION AND DECISION MAKING

In the health care context, marriage conveys a number of state-specific rights, most especially the ability to have access to and make medical decisions for your spouse without anyone questioning or challenging your authority.

Before legally recognized marriages, same-sex couples needed documents demonstrating our intention to have our partner by our side in the event of a medical crisis, to have our partner provide doctors with much-needed information, and to have our partner make medical decisions. Without these documents, health care providers can tell LGBT people that only family members have rights. Medical drama is already difficult. To have to endure it without support from the person you love most adds insult to injury.

When estate planning was the only way to bring legitimacy under the law to our relationships, many gay and lesbian people took the time and spent the money to create the necessary documents. Estate planning, as discussed in more detail in Chapter 9, generally consists of wills, trusts, and advance directives. Advance directives include a document that tells health care providers who your designee is and orders that they should treat the designee like a spouse. This document is called different things in different states, including health care power of attorney, health care proxy, designation of health care surrogate, and other titles. Now, of course, your designee can actually *be* your spouse. Instead of a trip to a lawyer, you can make a trip down the aisle.

William and Alan's Story

....

As we've seen, William and Alan were in a loving, committed relationship and saw no reason to complicate matters by marrying. Then one day Alan had a heart attack. When the couple arrived at the hospital, the nurse asked William what their relationship was, and he proudly stated that they were lovers and that he would be by Alan's side throughout the ordeal. Unfortunately, that statement was not enough; Alan was unconscious at this point and unable to state his own wishes. Without being able to assure the nurses that he had legal authority, by virtue of marriage or a valid health care power of attorney, William was left to sit outside in the waiting room while a nurse tried to locate a "family member." The nurse finally reached Alan's homophobic mother, who instructed the health care providers to ignore William, whom she believed had forced her son to be gay; she told the nurse that she would be on the next flight in and would assume complete charge. The nurse did as her hospital's risk management department advised her and heeded the mother's wishes. Alan's mother swooped in and took over his medical care, inviting William to not let the door hit him in the butt on his way out.

Marriage has its benefits. Among them are not being questioned in a health crisis situation and having your relationship recognized when it most matters.

Even when you are married, it is still important to have that health care surrogate (or health care proxy, or power of attorney, or whatever your state calls the document that specifies who should have access to you and authority to make health care decisions for you). A living will is also critical should you be in an end-stage or terminal condition and wish to refuse any extraordinary life-sustaining treatment. Your spouse might not automatically be the decision maker if you cannot communicate for yourself. In some states, a spouse simply falls into the general category of "family member," and family members are the priority group authorized to make decisions. Thus it is better to have your intentions clearly stated to prevent a showdown in the hospital room between your significant other and your mother. Even if your state does grant a spouse automatic deference for health care decision making, consider what could happen if an accident occurs while you are traveling in a state that does not give you that right. Get it in writing! You can also expect homophobic or just uneducated health care providers to request proof that you are married (as if your parents carried around their marriage license). I keep a scanned copy of mine available on my mobile devices.

It cannot be emphasized enough: on all of these documents (and on all things where you are choosing a decision maker or beneficiary), be sure a second individual is named as an alternate to your primary designee and that all of the second individual's contact details are provided. In the event that you two are in an accident together, or if you or your partner is traveling, ill, or otherwise unable to get to the other, it is critical that you name a backup who can leap into action. Naming a secondary designee is reason enough to have advance directive documents, although this reason is frequently overlooked. I frequently see documents done using inexpensive online services, or even with an attorney, that name only a primary designee. Having a plan B in place is always important.

BURIAL AND CREMATION

Mortality is no fun to think about. But imagine how awful it would feel if, in addition to grieving over your loss, you could not make the decision as to where and how your partner's body should be laid to rest. As a legal spouse and, therefore, next of kin, you have the exclusive right to act in this capacity, and generally the authority of the deceased person's spouse will not be questioned. Still, burial and cremation have long been an issue in our community; too often, funeral homes would insist on calling our families of origin to get consent to bury or cremate our loved ones. Therefore, it is advisable to have your and your partner's specific intentions in writing so that your wishes are clear. This is typically done as part of the estate planning process. I usually prepare a separate statement of intention as to what should happen to one's bodily remains and have it executed with the same formalities as a will. I generally do not include those provisions in the will, so that if the will itself is locked in some safe deposit box somewhere that we need a court order to get to, the burial or cremation need not wait until the will is accessed. Feel free to get creative and specific about how you would want any service or celebration of your life to go down; I have had clients detail the music that should be played, flowers that should and should not be present (read: no carnations!), and much more. This is your final chance to produce an event in your life, so include your requests for dim lighting and poetry, or whatever else you want.

No section on spousal rights at death would be complete without mentioning the right to be listed as the surviving spouse on our beloved's death certificate. That is the very fight that took Jim Obergefell all the way from his small town in Ohio to the Supreme Court of the United States: he simply wanted his deceased husband's marital status to be entered correctly on his death certificate.

INHERITANCE

If you have an estate plan, you can determine who gets what when you die. If you do not have a plan, the state provides one for you. Your plan is usually outlined in a will or a trust, and on any accounts or assets for which you have designated beneficiaries or which are jointly owned; in fact, on accounts with beneficiaries in place or joint ownership, the assets go to those individuals regardless of whatever else is in place.

Each state has rules about inheritance. While they vary in specifics, there are a few principles that are nearly universal. If you have a valid will, your property goes to the person(s) detailed in the will in the proportions you have specified (subject to a few exceptions such as the elective share, explained below). Should you have no will or other testamentary document such as a trust, you die intestate, and your assets go to the person whom the law decides is your default heir. Your legally wedded spouse is always the first person in that line, followed by children, parents, siblings, and then other, more distant relatives. If you are married and die without a will, your spouse gets everything, unless you have children either from a prior relationship or from the current one, in which case the spouse and children divide the estate. If you do not want your spouse to get everything that would otherwise pass to him, make sure you have the documentation in place to modify that default. If you have anyone for whom you want to provide after your death, be aware that without a will, trust, or another testamentary disposition, such as having someone named as a co-owner or a beneficiary on your accounts, your spouse will get all assets that are in your name alone and which do not have a beneficiary designated already.

The elective share is important to understand, particularly if you are concerned about making provisions for people other than your spouse in your estate plan. It allows a surviving spouse to claim a portion of a deceased spouse's estate regardless of whether the will gives the surviving spouse less or even nothing at all. This elective share has been known historically as "dower" (rights that a wife could claim in the estate of a husband) or "curtesy" (rights that the husband could claim in the property of a wife). Elective share, discussed later in the context of prenuptial agreements, is the more modern, gender-neutral way to ensure that the surviving spouse is not disinherited. Typically the amount that a surviving spouse can elect against her deceased partner's estate is between a third and a half. The elective share is not automatically provided; the surviving spouse must petition the court to exercise this right. All states but Georgia have some form of an elective share. The nature of community property means that the nine states that adhere to that regime (Arizona, California, Idaho, Louisiana, Nevada, New Mexico, Texas, Washington, and Wisconsin) presume that a surviving spouse gets half of any community property that belongs to them, plus a share of your community property share, despite any provisions in a will to the contrary. All of the other states (again, aside from Georgia) grant a surviving spouse automatic rights to inherit from a deceased spouse's estate. Georgia is the lone outlier; there the law provides just a year of support for a surviving spouse.

Jackie and Lisa's Story

••••••••••

Jackie and Lisa have been together for several years when they decide to get married. Jackie has two kids from her prior heterosexual marriage to a nice guy named Steve. Jackie and Steve are co-parenting well, and Lisa is a good stepmom. Five years after they marry, Jackie gets diagnosed with inoperable metastatic cancer. She never considered seeing a lawyer to draw up a prenuptial agreement or a will, believing that her daughters would get everything she wants them to have, per her explicitly stated wishes to Lisa and everyone else. She tells Lisa that she wants everything—all of her assets—to go to her kids, and Lisa agrees. After Jackie's death, Lisa decides that the children will not need all of their mom's assets, since Steve is perfectly able to take care of them with his income. Lisa gets half of the estate and Jackie's daughters get the other half because of the laws of intestacy, which apply when one is legally married and dies without a will. Under the intestacy statute of the state where Jackie died, which is basically similar to that of most other states, children from a prior relationship only get half of the estate and the other half passes to the surviving spouse. This is not what Jackie wanted, but it is what the law provides, absent a properly executed nuptial agreement and an estate plan providing otherwise. Lisa and Jackie's kids split all of Jackie's assets in half. That may well mean some messed-up karma for Lisa, but it's cold comfort for Jackie's children, who have now lost a mom, a stepmom, and half of the assets that their mom wanted them to have. Marriage does not make people better, more trustworthy people, and it sure did not do that for Lisa. Jackie needed to have documented her wishes through a will or a trust.

ESTATE AND GIFT TAX

One of the major benefits of marriage for higher-net-worth couples is the estate tax and gift tax exemption to married couples. Absent some sort of exception, the tax code generally places a tax on any transfer of assets from one person to another over a certain amount of money. However, the tax code makes a critical exception—the right of one spouse to pass an unlimited amount of assets tax free to the other spouse, provided she is a U.S. citizen. This is known as the "unlimited marital deduction," and it allows a married couple to freely treat the assets of each as part of the family's assets if they choose to,

STATES WITH INHERITANCE OR ESTATE TAX

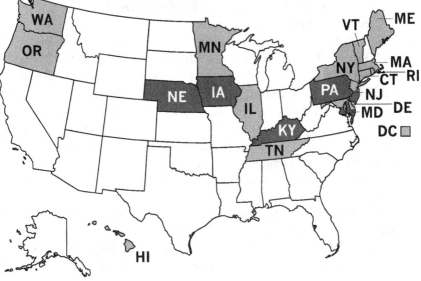

 STATES WITH AN ESTATE TAX:
Connecticut, Delaware, District of Columbia, Hawaii, Illinois, Maine, Massachusetts, Minnesota, New York, Oregon, Rhode Island, Tennessee, Vermont, and Washington

 STATES WITH AN INHERITANCE TAX:
Iowa, Kentucky, Nebraska, and Pennsylvania

New Jersey and Maryland residents are subject to both an estate tax and an inheritance tax.

without concern for the tax implications. This deduction is a big deal because otherwise the tax rate for these transfers is astounding.

As a very public example, consider the plaintiff in the lawsuit that took down the core of DOMA, Edie Windsor. Because her marriage was not considered valid by the federal government or her home state of New York, she had to pay a federal estate tax bill at the death of her spouse of over $363,000. In addition, because New York is one of the jurisdictions that has a state estate or inheritance tax, she also was saddled with a tax burden of over $275,500 payable to New York State's taxing authority.

Currently the states with an estate tax are Connecticut, Delaware, the District of Columbia, Hawaii, Illinois, Maine, Maryland, Massachusetts, Minnesota, New Jersey, New York, Oregon, Rhode Island, Tennessee, Vermont, and Washington. These jurisdictions all have a marital deduction similar to the federal one: when a married person dies, she can give her spouse an unlimited amount tax free. The states with an inheritance tax currently are Iowa, Kentucky, Maryland, Nebraska, New Jersey, and Pennsylvania; each of these states exempts from any tax property inherited from a deceased spouse.

This boon to our families' bottom lines is why, for many years, when folks would ask me if I was pushing for the freedom to marry, I would exclaim that having that right would be lovely, but what I really wanted for our community was the unlimited marital deduction (and divorce, too)!

William and Alan's Story

•••••••••••••

Let's return to William and his beloved, Alan. When Alan recovered from his heart attack, they decided that they would elope in order to prevent anything like that hospital hell from happening again. And that was a good thing, because less than a year after their marriage, Alan had a second heart attack. This time the damage to the heart was more serious, and Alan died.

William was left to deal with the couple's assets. Once the properties in Fire Island and Fort Lauderdale were sold, and the retirement accounts and insurance policy were tallied, Alan had a sizable estate, close to $7 million. If the couple had not been legally married, William would have had to pay taxes on everything above Alan's lifetime exemption amount, which in the year of Alan's death was $5.35 million. And at a tax rate of almost 55 percent, that could have been close to $1 million.

Instead, because they were married, William was able to take the marital deduction. He kept all of the money he inherited from Alan, paying zero in estate or gift tax. With all of those savings, William was able to make significant charitable donations in Alan's name—to the progressive charities his mother-in-law hated the most.

Now, when you read "estate," you might be thinking that applies only to people with huge amounts of money or property. As of 2016, the amount that can be passed during one's lifetime to a nonspouse is $5.45 million; accountants, tax preparers, and attorneys call this the "lifetime exemption amount" or "applicable exclusion amount." Yes, that is a lot of money, but between real estate, retirement accounts, and life insurance proceeds paid out at death, the value of an estate can add up quickly. You need not be a Doris Duke kind of heiress to enjoy the estate tax benefits for married couples.

For example, before marriage equality, one issue that LGBT couples struggled with was how to pass property to their partner at death. Suppose that you have a condo that you purchased before you and your sweetie fell in love. Now you want to add your partner's name to the title so that he would get it at your death; adding your partner to the title is a gift of half of the assessed value of the condo. Prior to federal recognition of our marriages, we had to worry about the gift tax consequences of that simple transaction. Say the condo is worth $150,000 and you still carry a $50,000 mortgage on it. The value of the condo is $100,000. If you add your partner's name, he receives a $50,000 gift from you. If the value of the property is in excess of the annual gift tax exclusion (currently $14,000 annually), as it is in our example, the balance—in this case, $36,000—becomes part of a lifetime gift tax exclusion (which, like the estate tax exclusion, is now $5.45 million). If an unmarried couple exceeds the $5.45 million, a hefty tax would be due on the overage once that amount was exceeded. But if a couple is legally married, the IRS treats that marriage as valid for all purposes, including estate and gift tax. That means that whatever you give to your spouse in life or at death below the lifetime gift tax exclusion is tax-free. You might have still done the transaction before being married, but you would have been eating into your lifetime exclusion; now you need not be worried about even filing a gift tax return, because if you are married, this is simply not a gift. Brilliant!

Marriage equality makes estate planning easier. There is less need for additional layers of creative estate and tax planning in order to avoid gift and estate taxes. Married same-sex couples can now plan like heterosexual couples. Same-sex couples no longer need to purchase pricey life insurance policies to pay onerous estate tax bills. Couples need not utilize complex trusts to make sure property passes to our partners or devise mechanisms such as promissory notes that are forgiven over time when adding one partner on the title to a property.

In addition, the applicable exclusion amount is now "portable" for married couples. This means that if your spouse does not use the lifetime exemption and you make the proper filing with the IRS at the death of your spouse, that $5.45 million amount becomes yours to use in your life through gifting and at your death. With the portable exclusion amount, surviving spouses can make greater lifetime gifts and bequests in estate plans without being subject to gift and estate tax because of the spouse's unused exemption. In 2016, this means that a surviving spouse could leave up to $10,900,000 at death free of estate tax.

Complex estate planning mechanisms such as Qualified Terminal Interest Property (QTIP) trusts or Qualified Domestic Trusts (QDOT) are now available to same-sex married couples. If you have children and/or have a high net worth, these tools can to help maximize the marital deduction and provide for loved ones.

QTIP trusts give a spouse the right to stay in a residence or utilize assets for her lifetime (a limited lifetime-only interest is known as a "life estate") and then at death pass the property to your children, a charity, siblings, or other beneficiaries. Property in a QTIP passes entirely free from estate tax because it benefits from the unlimited marital deduction. If this is a mutual intention (both of you want your assets to benefit the spouse during her lifetime but then pass to someone else at her death), you can each do a QTIP trust and the trust assets are not subject to estate tax until the surviving spouse dies. The QTIP trust's life estate can only benefit a spouse who is a U.S. citizen. There are restrictions on what your spouse can do with the property after your death: she cannot sell or transfer it during her lifetime.

Like a QTIP, a QDOT allows a non-U.S.-citizen spouse to take advantage of the marital deduction, typically available only to U.S. citizen spouses. The QDOT also has various restrictions, including who the trustee can be and how the funds can be spent. The income from the funds in the QDOT trust can be used for the surviving noncitizen spouse's lifetime needs, and she pays income tax, not estate tax, on what she receives. The principal can be invaded only for certain emergency needs. The ultimate beneficiaries pay the estate tax at the death of the noncitizen spouse to the extent that the amount remaining is above the lifetime exemption, meaning that more funds were available for the support of the noncitizen spouse in her life. Remember, we are talking about $5.45 million now; there have to be numbers deserving of this level of planning and restriction of funds for your noncitizen spouse.

If you already had an estate plan in place and are marrying or have married subsequent to the plan's creation, consider whether you want to make any changes. For example, many couples with substantial estates beyond the exemption had made plans to give their partners an amount up to that applicable exclusion amount and then everything else to a charity in order that the overage would not be subject to estate tax at a rate that has historically been as high as 50 percent. Now that a same-sex married couple can take advantage of that unlimited marital deduction, plans might be revisited to simply give everything to your spouse (do not forget about those charitable intentions, though!) and to also take advantage of any lifetime gifting that you might have wanted to do.

Lifetime gifting helps others and reduces the overall size of your estate. You and your U.S. citizen spouse can combine your annual gift tax exclusion in what is known as gift splitting. In 2016, each person gets an exclusion of $14,000 per year per recipient. Married couples can combine their annual exclusions to make gifts of larger amounts. This means that if you and your spouse wish to give $28,000 to your nephew as a gift, you can elect for that gift to be attributed equally to each of you. That way, you—and the recipient—pay no tax on the gift because it is within the annual amount you each are permitted to give to someone.

An important note for people with recently deceased partners: If you have just paid estate tax on the death of your spouse because the marriage was not recognized, but the marriage subsequently became legally recognized, talk to your accountant about whether you can reopen the return and seek a refund of the tax paid.

PROPERTY OWNERSHIP

In most states, there are two ways to own property jointly as an unmarried couple: as joint tenants with rights of survivorship, and through tenancy in common. Married couples also can own property through tenancy by the entireties.

Joint Tenants with Rights of Survivorship

Before marriage equality, many same-sex couples owned property as joint tenants with rights of survivorship. In this form of ownership, each owner holds an undivided interest in the whole property. This ownership can be severed by either tenant, as sometimes can happen in an acrimonious breakup. Also, a creditor of either owner can place a lien or otherwise encumber the whole property. At the death of one, the property passes automatically to the survivor without going through the court-based estate administration process known as probate.

Tenancy in Common

Tenancy in common is how property is jointly held when there is no specific mention in the deed of a right of survivorship. Tenants in common each own half of the property unless the deed allocates different shares. At the death of one owner, her share passes according to her will (or, absent one, via the laws of intestacy) to her beneficiaries. This type of ownership can create problems for unmarried same-sex couples without a will—family members could force the sale of the property.

Tenancy by the Entireties

Tenancy by the entireties is how married couples own property in many states, and this form of ownership provides much-deserved protection. There are two primary benefits to owning property this way: enhanced protection against the claims of creditors, and enhanced protection against each other. A creditor of one spouse cannot encumber the property unless the debt belongs to both spouses, which is not too common. Also, the tenancy cannot be severed unless both members of the married couple consent. Shortly after marriage equality came to our shores, I received a rush of inquiries from folks who wanted to retitle their properties and accounts so that they could take advantage of the asset protection aspects of tenancy by the entireties.

Homestead Protections

In addition to the method of ownership, it is important to consider the concept of homestead, if that is a factor in your state. Homestead refers to the way in which a primary residence is protected from the claims of creditors, from being taken away at death, and from a sharp uptick in property taxes as its value increases.

Some states stipulate that if your residence is your homestead, it cannot be left to anyone in your will or trust except your spouse, unless there is an agreement waiving spousal priority. In some states it is not an option to oust a spouse from homestead absent a written waiver of that right. If your will says that your home goes to your children (who are not the legal children of your spouse) with the understanding that your wife will be fine on her own, that provision might fail if challenged in court, whether or not you are leaving money for her to relocate.

The same restriction could apply in selling a homestead property: if you are married, you must have your spouse's consent to do so. This consent is required even if the property was purchased solely with your own funds and is in your own name. A pre- or postnuptial agreement can modify this default.

Property tax protections are something to consider when getting married. If your state allows for homestead exemptions, which essentially freeze the value of the residence, property taxes stay level and do not increase in proportion to the rising fair market value of the home. This is a real savings if your home has appreciated in value over the years. Without a homestead exemption to cap property taxes, those taxes can be even more onerous. Some same-sex couples have kept separate legal residences so that each can have a homestead property and take advantage both of being legal strangers to each other and of the property tax cap. Married couples typically cannot, however, have two homesteads. If your choice to marry means that you will lose one homestead exemption, exercise caution and understand the implications of marriage in your situation.

Homestead protections are a stellar benefit of marriage, one that

JOINT OWNERSHIP OF REAL PROPERTY

There are three different forms of joint ownership: tenants in common, joint tenants with rights of survivorship, and tenants by the entireties.

	TIC	JTWROS	TBE
Can be co-owned by more than two parties	●	●	●
Is only available to married couples			●
Can own unequal shares in property (for example, 60/40 or 25/25/50)	●		
Each party owns an equal and undivided interest in the property (100%)		●	
The parties, as a marital unit, own an undivided interest in the property (100%)			●
Any party can sell or mortgage their interest in the property without the consent of any other co-owners (though the buyer or mortgagor may insist on written consent of all co-owners)	●	●	
The spouses must jointly agree on selling or mortgaging the property			●
A creditor of any individual co-owner can attach to the property and force a sale	●	●	
In order to attach to the property and force a sale, a creditor must be a creditor of both spouses			●
When one co-owner dies, his interest passes to his heirs at law according to his will or the laws of intestacy, and not to the other co-owner(s)	●		
When one co-owner dies, her interest in the property automatically passes to the remaining co-owner(s)		●	●

Please note: Some states allow certain qualifying properties to be deemed "homestead," which would grant additional protections not listed above.

advocates repeatedly articulated during our battle for marriage equality. I had a client whose spouse died just before his marriage was recognized in Florida. They co-owned their home, but the spouse who died was the original owner, with the other spouse's name having been added to the title later. The homestead exemption died with the original property owner because under Florida law at the time there was no "surviving spouse." My client's property taxes went from $6,000 to $60,000 overnight; he could not afford this higher tax bill and was forced to sell his home.

RETIREMENT ASSETS

For same-sex couples, handling retirement assets is one of the triumphs of marriage equality. If you have retirement assets, yay for you! Marriage equality means you are able to roll over your spouse's retirement account to yours or another eligible retirement account at death, tax free, and maintain it on the same favorable tax and distribution terms as your own; previously, same-sex surviving spouses were forced to take out the whole amount at death and pay taxes on it.

The rolled-over accounts do not require withdrawals until you are age 70½. This requirement to withdraw, called the required minimum distribution (or RMD), is stretched out for married couples: you have to begin taking distributions from your retirement account only once the younger of you turns age 70½. You can stretch those RMDs out for payments from your own retirement account, which you might want to do to maintain yourself in a lower tax bracket. Also, in many cases, a rolled-over retirement account has greater creditor protection than an inherited account; for example, a rolled-over IRA is protected from creditors upon bankruptcy, whereas inherited IRAs have greater exposure.

The handling of retirement assets is complex and is governed by both federal and state laws. If your spouse passes away, take the time to consult with professionals about how to handle the retirement accounts. For instance, if you roll over his IRA into your own IRA, then discover that you need access to those funds, you will pay the standard penalty of 10 percent for withdrawals before you reach age 59½. Younger widowers might consider just leaving the account as is (intact and in the name of your deceased spouse), because you need not withdraw anything until your spouse would have been 70½.

If you have already designated your partner on your beneficiary designation form and later decide to marry, change the type of relationship to "spouse." Call up the company that manages your retirement account or log in to its website and request a change in beneficiary classification. This ensures that you can take advantage of the aforementioned spousal benefits such as rollover, stretched-out RMDs, and enhanced creditor protection.

Marriage also has an advantage when it comes to pensions. "Pension" here refers to the retirement benefits provided by governments and other nonprofits. They are generally either a "defined benefit," where the contributions are mostly made by the employer, or a "defined contribution," where the employee's earnings constitute the majority of the contributions (and are often matched by the employer). Prior to marriage equality, for the most part, we could not pass our pensions to our same-sex partners unless we were in legally recognized marriages. While there are exceptions, many pensions require the beneficiary to be a minor child or a legally wedded spouse. Many same-sex couples have had to forfeit large chunks of their pension benefits because they had no spousal beneficiary. To mitigate this challenge, many people elected a lump sum payout from their pension. For people with a normal life expectancy, taking the monthly payments over time usually results in a larger overall payout than a lump sum disbursement, but without the option to leave the pension to a legally recognized spouse, gay and lesbian employees had few options and certainly left a lot of pension funds on the table.

For example, I had a client whose partner had worked as a police officer and died suddenly. My client was the designee on his partner's pension through work. Each quarter the statement would come to their home, and while on the front side it said that the client was the designated beneficiary, on the back side it said that the beneficiary had to be what was termed a "joint annuitant," which meant a spouse or a child under the age of twenty-five. We challenged the discriminatory nature of that provision, but given both that these terms were clearly indicated on every statement and that the law did not recognize same-sex relationships, we failed to win our appeal, and my client ended up with nothing—zero.

If you are legally married, be sure that your designation-of-beneficiary form makes clear that the designee is your spouse. There are often specific elections you have to make in order for your spouse to qualify for the benefit, especially as you near retirement. Certain financial advisors are especially versed in the appropriate selections to make on these forms; consult with an experienced professional. Sometimes, once a selection is made, the ship has sailed and no changes can be made; in these cases it is critical to get it right from the first instance. If you made an election before marriage and/or before your marriage was recognized by your state, you might be unable to change the election. The IRS has recognized that such amendments would be challenging to implement, particularly if you have already retired. Get specific advice about that issue.

Another potential issue is that many plans have spousal consent rules. Spousal consent requires that any spouse who is not intended to be the beneficiary of a retirement account must execute a written waiver evidencing that understanding. A loan from a retirement plan may also require written spousal consent before withdrawal is allowed. The Employee Retirement Income Security Act of 1974 (ERISA) is the set of government rules that applies to most private employer-sponsored health insurance benefits and retirement accounts such as 401(k) plans. ERISA requires that any waivers of spousal retirement benefits after the date of the marriage be in writing. Review those retirement account beneficiary designations, and if you are excluding your spouse for whatever reason, have her execute the necessary written confirmation of that waiver.

If you signed after you married and listed a nonspouse beneficiary without written consent of the spouse, the designation may be deemed invalid and therefore fail.

Jackie and Lisa's Story

••••••••••

Remember Jackie and Lisa? Jackie wanted her children to inherit from her; she named them on her retirement account as the beneficiaries. Jackie and

Lisa married without a prenuptial agreement. Jackie could have reached out to her financial advisor or whoever helps manage her retirement accounts to obtain the waiver form on which Lisa consents to Jackie naming others as the beneficiaries of this asset. Without a prenuptial agreement or a consent document in place, when Jackie died, Lisa chose to override Jackie's designation of her daughters and usurped that account for her own benefit.

Hardship withdrawals are another benefit available to married same-sex couples. Some retirement accounts, usually 401(k)s, allow the account owner to withdraw funds for unforeseeable emergencies such as medical or funeral expenses or to repair a damaged home. You must prove that there are no other assets to satisfy the obligation, and, unlike a loan, the amount cannot be repaid; it permanently depletes the account. The amount taken out through hardship withdrawals can be up to one-half of your account balance or $50,000, whichever is lower, but there's a 10 percent penalty for the withdrawal, which must be paid to the IRS when you file your taxes. Be sure it is an emergency for which no other funds are available. Also, know that you are not allowed to make elective contributions to the account for a six-month period after the withdrawal.

If it would be advantageous to have ERISA govern your retirement accounts versus the IRS, consider transferring your IRA assets into a 401(k).

Jackie and Lisa's Story

• • • • • • • • • • •

As Jackie's cancer was advancing, Lisa wanted to withdraw funds from her own retirement account to keep the bills paid while she stayed home and cared for Jackie. She would not have been able to do that before they married because Jackie was not considered "family." Because they were married, however, she was able to complete the required forms and provide evidence of the emergency need for funds, so she was able to make that withdrawal.

FAMILY AND MEDICAL LEAVE ACT

The Family and Medical Leave Act (FMLA) applies to employers who regularly employ fifty or more people. Under FMLA, if a full-time employee who has been at the job for more than a year and has worked at least 1,250 hours in that year needs to take off time to care for a spouse, the employer must keep her job or its equivalent available. Typically the employee can take twelve weeks off per year for such a purpose. FMLA leave is unpaid. If you or your spouse need to take time off from work to care for each other or for a family member, it can be a great relief to know that you will still have a job on the flip side. The leave can be used for one's own illness or that of another family member, for post-birth bonding, after taking in a foster or adoptive child, or to care for a sick child. Before marriage equality, we were not able to take advantage of FMLA leave to care for our partners. The twelve weeks of unpaid leave expands to twenty-six weeks when you have an eligible spouse who is suffering a serious injury or illness and needs your care.

WRONGFUL DEATH CLAIMS

If you lose your partner to medical malpractice or an injury for which another person is responsible, being married means you have the legal right to bring an action in court for that loss. In many states, the claim will be for a "loss of consortium," the legal term for the damage from the death of a spouse due to the injury wrongfully caused by another. Absent a marriage, courts typically deny the surviving partner the ability to sue (known as "legal standing"). Being married means you will have the authority to bring an action in the place of your deceased beloved and hold accountable those liable for her death. Suing for your loss could both help bring justice after the death of your spouse and provide monetary support you will most likely need.

ALIMONY FROM A PRIOR MARRIAGE

Marriage impacts those who were married previously in ways that deserve careful analysis. If you were married and are receiving spousal support, which usually terminates upon a subsequent marriage, look into whether it is legally and financially significant and worthwhile to refrain from marrying again. It is important to understand your rights and obligations under your previous divorce decree. Some agreements and states have specific prohibitions against retaining your alimony or subject you to reduced alimony if you are cohabitating in a "supportive relationship," as that is deemed unfair to the spouse who is paying your alimony. No eating your cake and having it, too. Sorry!

SPOUSAL PRIVILEGE

Spousal privilege, sometimes called spousal immunity, applies in both criminal and civil cases. Subject to a few exceptions, a spouse cannot be forced to testify against a spouse, and any communications made to one's spouse are protected as confidential. Spousal privilege survives divorce and death. Either party can assert the privilege. If your wife does not want to testify about something that you said during a conversation that was just between the two of you, with no one else present, she cannot be compelled to testify. If she does, however, want to testify against you about that conversation—say, after you have split up—you can claim the privilege prevents her from doing so.

GOVERNMENTAL EMPLOYEES AND CONTRACTORS ETHICS STANDARDS

Same-sex married couples in which one or both spouses are governmental employees or contractors now must comply with the ethics standards for married couples. If either you or your honey work for the government in any capacity, consider the wide-ranging potential impact of marriage. Depending on the department or division, federal and state governments have varying and substantial rules and regulations regarding certain kinds of behaviors that their employees and contractors can and cannot engage in. Upon marriage, those same ethics standards expose the non-government-employee spouse to a whole new world of limits. In some cases these restrictions apply even after leaving employment. These rules ensure that there is no appearance of impropriety or inappropriate use of influence. For example, the giving of gifts or ownership of stocks can raise the specter of conflicts of interest. I cannot send a holiday gift basket to the adoption court clerk who is helpful to me year-round unless it is sent to her at work and addressed to and shared with her whole division. Imagine if I had a separate friendship with that clerk's girlfriend. Their getting married means my relationship with my pal just shifted, and I need to be careful about buying birthday gifts and meals for her to avoid any ethical violations.

5
DO YOU "I DO" OR DON'T YOU?

Marriage is a fine institution, but I'm not ready for an institution.

—*Mae West*

We have fought hard for marriage equality. We deserve the fundamental right to wed the partner of our choice. Still, as we have known for many decades, LGBT people build stable, loving, committed relationships without marriage. Several studies show that today fewer heterosexual couples are choosing to marry, deeming marriage an outmoded, musty institution. The irony is not lost on us that as many straight folks have been bailing from the marital ship, gay couples have clamored to jump aboard. Maybe after the thrill of marriage equality wanes, more same-sex couples will regard marriage the same way some younger heterosexual couples do: as not much more than a "piece of paper."

CHOOSING NOT TO GET HITCHED

Couples, gay and straight, who can marry, may choose not to marry for a variety of reasons. Some feel they have been off the grid for so long that they are comfortable there. Another reason is that monogamy and fidelity, which are often part of a marriage agreement and an integral part of ceremonial language at many weddings, are not central to everyone's idea of committed relationships. As filmmaker

John Waters put it back in 2007, referencing the movements both for marriage equality and to repeal the ban against gay people serving openly in the military: "I always thought the privilege of being gay is that we do not have to get married or go in the Army. I personally have no desire to imitate a fairly corny, expensive heterosexual tradition, though I certainly know gay couples who are married who should be. I am all for it. I have always joked that the growth industries are gay divorce and tattoo removal."

Some couples do not see the benefits of marriage as outweighing the potential risks. I have often heard altar-shy clients in my office wonder aloud why one should attempt to fix something that is not broken. Some people have been burned in the past by relationships that ended badly. Some folks have parents who stayed in an awful marriage; other folks have heard horror stories from friends or co-workers about unhappy marriages and messy divorces. Some people place prudence above romance and do not like the financial consequences of marriage, such as automatic rights on death and divorce. A mundane but major development in reasons not to marry comes from the greater availability of health insurance in the United States. Before the expansion of access to health insurance in the United States, some people married in order to receive employer-provided health insurance through their spouse. Other anti-marriage stories offer the punch line of great relationships being ruined by marriage. I gave a talk at which one attendee who was going through his own marital dissolution quipped that the leading cause of divorce is marriage.

TOP TEN REASONS SAME-SEX COUPLES MIGHT CHOOSE NOT TO MARRY

There are lots of good reasons not to marry. Here are the top ten reasons I have heard.

1. *Automatic rights on divorce.* Absent a prenuptial agreement, your spouse could be entitled to alimony if you

separate. Also, she could claim that she is due half of everything earned in the marriage. This includes increases in the value of property and accounts you owned before the marriage. Prenuptial agreements done by attorneys who are experienced in this area should be enforceable—though some property and support rights may not be waivable in some states—but some people simply prefer to remain unmarried.

2. *Automatic rights of inheritance.* Absent a will or trust, your spouse inherits all of the assets in your name at your death. If you have a will providing for your children, your spouse still has an elective share by law. That means he can choose to take a third or more of the estate, regardless of your stated intentions. That elective share can be addressed and waived in a prenuptial agreement.

3. *Income taxes.* If you decide to marry, even if you are not big earners (and perhaps especially if you are not), you could end up getting hit with a bigger tax bill from the IRS because of the marriage penalty. The marriage penalty usually is triggered when both spouses have similar incomes. A taxpayer's spouse cannot be a dependent of the taxpayer, and for some couples the dependent exemption is a better benefit than filing jointly as a married couple. Talk to your tax advisor if your partner does not work and see if he is eligible to be claimed as a dependent, and whether that may be more tax advantageous than marriage.

4. *Adoption tax credit.* This credit is substantial. It offsets the costs of adopting a child unrelated to you or your partner. It also offsets the cost of second-parent adoptions (when you adopt a child who legally belongs to your partner by birth or adoption); however, you cannot use the adoption tax credit if you are married to your partner and obtaining a stepparent adoption. Some parents choose to first handle a legal second-parent adoption and then marry to maximize the tax benefits, taking the risk

that they are unprotected until after an adoption. For higher-income households, the tax credit may not be available: it begins to phase out for those with incomes over $201,010, who can take only a partial credit, and families with incomes over $241,010 are entirely ineligible for the credit.

5. *SSI.* Married individuals generally receive less together on Supplemental Security Income (SSI), a form of government assistance for elderly or disabled individuals, than they do individually. If you are on a benefits program that determines your benefit by looking at your income and assets, be aware that marriage might reduce your monthly benefit payments. For example, couples who are both receiving SSI will receive roughly one-quarter less as a married couple than they would receive as two individuals living together. And couples where one is receiving SSI and the other is not will, upon marriage, face a review of the assets and income of the spouse not receiving SSI to be sure that any resources that could support the household are being used to do so; that could reduce the benefits to which the eligible spouse is entitled, or eliminate them altogether.

6. *Medicaid.* Medicaid provides health and long-term-care insurance coverage for low-income people. Getting married might impact that benefit because eligibility is based on household income and assets. Look at whether marriage will disqualify you from Medicaid.

7. *Medicare.* Medicare is a health insurance benefit for people over sixty-five years old or with certain disabilities. Premiums are determined by several factors, including work history, income, and resources. Marriage can increase premiums because another person's income and resources are included in the calculations, and lesser assistance might be available as a result of marriage.

8. *Payments (and benefits) from a prior spouse.* If you or your partner were previously married and are receiving al-

imony that terminates upon a subsequent marriage, consider whether it is worthwhile to refrain from remarriage. Note that some states have restrictions against retaining your spousal support at its current level if you are cohabitating in a "supportive relationship," as it is deemed unfair to the spouse who is paying your alimony. Also, if you were married to someone for more than ten years and you currently collect Social Security on that former spouse, you forfeit that if you marry your current partner before age sixty. This may serve as an incentive to delay or forgo marriage if those benefits are significant to you.

9. *Other pooled income consequences.* There are other various ways that having another income in your family can create unintended negative consequences. For example, the subsidies known as Advance Premium Tax Credits, which bring down your premiums for insurance on the Affordable Care Act's marketplace exchange, are lower if your household income is higher. Similarly, your payments on student loans might be higher because of the increased household income, which must be disclosed.

10. *Ick!* No list about potential reasons to stay unmarried would be complete without a mention that there are those who are politically and philosophically opposed to marriage on its face. Whether because marriage has historically been a patriarchal, exclusive, and oppressive institution or because of a desire to have less government involvement in our lives and relationships, not everyone is gung-ho on marriage. That is okay, too!

These are all valid reasons why you might choose not to marry. Eschewing marriage need not signal any lack of lifelong commitment to being together, in sickness and in health, for richer or for poorer. While the first nine hesitations have the thread of financial concerns, the final one represents a political perspective. Many feminist voices in our movement continue to agitate for change to the institution itself. They maintain that marriage is not the be-all and end-all for family recognition. These values, deeply embedded in the LGBT movement, deserve continued consideration and ought to be understood by those readers newer to queer activist history who both might take marriage for granted and assume that we have all been on the same page with regard to the marriage fight from the get–go.

Marriage has been seen by many in the LGBT community as a problematic goal, one that has consumed outsize resources yet failed to change a system of privileging a traditional relationship model at the expense of denying a constellation of various family structures. While marriage is not a one-size-fits-all-our-diverse-families institution, it is one we ought to have access to, and we celebrate achieving that right, albeit with hesitation.

Working Through the Pain of Discrimination

CAROL BUELL

Attorney and mediator

Weiss, Buell & Bell

New York, New York

Over the past four years I have had hundreds of conversations with my clients about marriage. I have borne witness to what feels like Elizabeth Kübler-Ross's five stages of grief as my clients work their way through their own forms of personal pain, denial, anger, bargaining, depression, and eventual acceptance of what marriage means to them personally, as a couple, and as a family.

Why do I associate marriage equality in the LGBTQ community with trauma and personal loss? Because we experience the pain together in our meetings, as my clients rail against the institution that shunned them and shed tears of anger and pain. We think back to the personal insults over the decades: being placed at the "singles" table at cousin Judy's wedding; having a conversation with our sister about our unwillingness to attend her wedding unless our partner is invited, only to find no invitation in the mail at all. We remember the years in which we intentionally avoid any wedding ceremonies because we could not stand being "in the closet" at one more event, and then our eventual outspoken boycott of every wedding, refusing to participate in any celebration that shuns our families. We think about the years of defining our own relationships in the absence of legal ties, proud that we have survived without the benefit of a wedding ring. Commitment? we say. Who has ever needed a ring to prove commitment? Why embrace a patriarchal institution? We do not need it!

And then I carefully talk about the real, pragmatic benefits of marriage. Are one partner's Social Security benefits significantly larger than the other's? Do you continue to be estranged from your siblings, who are your legal next of kin, and could one of them contest your will, even though you have lived with your beloved partner for the last forty years? We talk about taxes, health care, end of life, cremation, nursing care, and children. We talk about all the benefits to which we would be entitled, in the same way anthropologists would discuss some strange and unknown culture from a foreign land, and get angry all over again. And eventually some of my clients decide there are benefits to joining this patriarchal institution, so they hold their noses and jump in.

But here is another source of pain and trauma: my clients fear the loss of a cultural identity which embraced "other," as the LGBTQ community brought together people as wide and varied as one's imagination. The only thing LGBTQ people had in common was their sexual orientation or sexual identity. They were LGBTQ *and* African American, Greek, WASP, polyamorous, evangelical, blue-collar, sex worker, investment banker, biker, Muslim.

Discrimination brought us together as a community. What will bring us together now?

Questioning the inclusivity of marriage equality as a goal has a long history. Some might remember the ovular work of the late, great Paula Ettelbrick, who warned that our movement's excessive focus on winning marriage equality would not bring justice to all but instead would force us into a mainstream mold that does not work for everyone. Paula got us thinking and talking about who gets left behind as we prioritize assimilation and put aside efforts to dismantle a status quo that limits freedom and hands over control of our families to the government.

Professor Nancy Polikoff also has been at the forefront of these conversations for more than four decades. She points out that if we could decouple some of the fifteen hundred rights and responsibilities from marriage and instead make them available to emotionally and financially interdependent people, we could create a more inclusive society grounded in the progressive feminist principles that protect everyone rather than leaving behind, for example, intergenerational relatives, single moms, people living nonmonogamously, and others who are, in point of fact, *family*.

Why the Law Shouldn't Value Marriage More Than Other Relationships . . . and Why I Chose It Anyway

NANCY D. POLIKOFF

Professor and attorney

Author, *Beyond (Straight and Gay) Marriage: Valuing All Families Under the Law*

American University Washington College of Law

Washington, D.C.

I never thought I would get married. Well, that's not exactly true. My high school boyfriend wanted to be a rabbi, and I did my share of doodling "Rabbi and Mrs.———" in my school notebooks. But before I came out, which happened when I was twenty-one, I became a radical feminist. I realized that marriage was a patriarchal institution that stripped women of their legal, social, and cultural autonomy and often hid violence and domination behind closed doors. No individual woman could fight the gender norms that permeated marriage. It was not for me. I joined a consciousness-raising group where I met the first lesbian mother I had ever known—a woman who lost custody of her children because of her sexual orientation.

I started law school in 1972, determined to fight for women's rights. I came out at the end of my first year. Gay liberation, like women's liberation, articulated new ideas about family and relationships. A year after graduating, I co-founded a feminist law collective and began a lifelong focus on family law. My feminist analysis deepened as I saw up close the persistence of gendered expectations, even after legal changes that were supposed to improve women's lives. I developed a specialty representing lesbian mothers. I went on to do feminist policy work on family law issues and eventually joined the faculty of the American University Washington College of Law, where I have taught for almost thirty years. My research, writing, and advocacy work has focused on gay and lesbian families, especially parents.

For many years, the lesbian feminists within the gay rights movement were united in advocating for redefined and expansive definitions of family. When gay men wanted to fight for same-sex marriage, we argued against making that a priority. Instead of fitting into the parameters of a deeply flawed institution, we wanted a new paradigm devoid of the historical baggage attached to marriage.

I remember receiving a phone call in 1988 or 1989 from Paula Ettelbrick, a staff lawyer at Lambda Legal with whom I had worked on many occasions. She told me she and the group's executive director, Tom Stoddard, were writing side-by-side essays reflecting the split among movement lawyers and activists on the subject of marriage. She ran her ideas past me and asked me to review her draft. I had no idea at the time, and neither did she, that those essays, which were originally published in *Out/Look* in the fall of 1989, would become iconic, memorializing competing LGBT visions of family for the subsequent decades.

Four years later a Hawaii court ruled, for the first time, that a ban on same-sex marriage would be unconstitutional unless the state could defend it by showing that it was necessary to achieve a compelling state interest. That court ruling marked the beginning of a new era, one in which, over time, the internal debate about fighting for marriage was eclipsed by the violent opposition of conservatives. In legislative struggles and numerous state ballot measures, there were only two options, one pro-gay and the other anti-gay. There was never a box to check in favor of a radical redefinition of family and relationships. In that way, I became a reluctant supporter of what came to be known as marriage equality.

But I never gave up on my belief that if marriage was to exist, it should not be special. Those organizing their primary relationships in other ways should get equal respect. What I knew best was the law, and so I wrote a book about why the law should not privilege marriage over other relationships. In *Beyond (Straight and Gay) Marriage: Valuing All Families Under the Law*, I argued for how to rewrite laws so that marriage was not the automatic dividing line between the relationships that were "in" and those that were "out." It is a vision I still passionately hold, one I hope will garner more support now that marriage equality is a nationwide reality.

Which brings me back to myself. I never thought I would get married. But I did. Cheryl, my partner of more than twenty years, was diagnosed with Parkinson's disease in 2008. We had registered as domestic partners in the District of Columbia in 2003, a status that gave us, locally, the rights and responsibilities of marriage. Although the District enacted marriage equality in 2009, we never considered it. After all, Cheryl, too, was a longtime radical feminist—an artist and producer, a founding member of the Los Angeles Women's Building and the Feminist Studio Workshop.

Then in early 2013, Cheryl expressed concern that I would leave her as her condition deteriorated. It was not fear of economic insecurity; our status as domestic partners gave her the right to share in my assets if we ever did separate. It was simply the fear that I would abandon her as too great a burden. It broke my heart to hear it. I assured her that I would not leave her, and I thought she believed me. Then a few weeks later she said it again.

And so it came to me that, although it was not rational, she might feel more secure if we married. Early on the morning of June 26, 2013, before the U.S. Supreme Court ruled that the federal Defense of Marriage Act was unconstitutional, I asked her to marry me. I timed it so that she would be clear that it was about my love for her and not the economic benefits that a federally recognized marriage would bring us. She said yes without hesitation.

And it turned out I was right. Marriage did not change our relationship. We are not one of those couples who wax eloquent about their relationship becoming more meaningful after they married. But it spoke to a place Cheryl was surprised to learn she had. Mostly she said that it was my willingness to marry her in spite of my principles that meant so much. The people who have known me and my work express surprise that I got married (although no one has expressed it quite as directly as my then thirty-year-old daughter, who screamed, "But you hate marriage!"). It turned out to be simple, though. The woman I love was suffering, and I found something that would lessen that. I did it with an open heart and without reservation.

Marriage holds a personal meaning for Cheryl and me. But it has not changed my views or lessened my disagreement with some of the arguments used to win marriage equality, those extolling marriage, setting it apart and ahead of all other human relationships. Justice Anthony Kennedy, writing the majority opinion in *Obergefell v. Hodges*, suggested that a life without marriage is a life of loneliness and that those without it are condemned to call out in the night and find no one there. That dismissal of unmarried relationships—including the one Cheryl and I had for more than twenty years—along with friendships, polyamorous arrangements, and intergenerational family connections does a disservice to the lives of so many people, gay and straight alike. When it becomes the basis for laws, it does an injustice to those lives. Long after marriage equality advocates pack up and go home, their mission accomplished, I plan to keep fighting that injustice.

Marriage is a contract—a social and legal contract. If you and your partner opt to marry, together the two of you enter into a contract with the state. Legislators at both the state and federal levels create laws that govern marriage and marital rights. If you and your partner do not want to opt in to the all-inclusive approach to marriage, you can decide to use an à la carte approach. If you wish to invoke particular rights and responsibilities for your committed relationship, seek competent counsel to advise you about the ways that you can protect each other with estate planning, contracts, and other available tools.

6
ALTERNATIVES TO MARRIAGE

I just never was the marrying kind.

—*Holland Taylor*

Before LGBT couples won the freedom to marry throughout the United States, our community achieved some meaningful substitutes in certain states, counties, and cities, including civil unions, domestic partnership registries, and reciprocal or designated beneficiaries. These relationship statuses are available still in some localities for couples choosing not to marry. In some places, these alternatives to marriage are only available to same-sex couples; in other places, different-sex couples can avail themselves of these forms of relationship recognition as well. These statuses confer different rights and responsibilities to couples. In some cases they give elements of marriage equivalence, but couples can only receive the federal benefits of marriage through legal marriage.

To date, the following jurisdictions have retained their marriage equivalent, either civil unions or domestic partnerships: California, Colorado, Hawaii, Illinois, New Jersey, Nevada, Oregon, and Washington, D.C. These statuses provide comprehensive state-based protections, including hospital visitation, inheritance, and the automatic rights associated with divorce. "Social Security Programs" in Chapter 4 reviews the Social Security Administration's position about the circumstances under which it will recognize nonmarital legal relationships as a marriage for the purposes of spousal death and retirement benefits. Still, those who entered into these statuses will now likely find that they no longer give them the greatest amount of protection available. For example, the Internal Revenue Service has specifically stated that it will not recognize civil unions or domestic partnerships for tax purposes, although it will recognize community property in states where civil union partners or domestic partners have community property.

Recognition of these alternatives to marriage is in flux and, in some cases, in jeopardy. Employers, states, and other entities that recognize them generally must treat these couples as married. In some states, corporations and institutions plan to phase out these benefits now that marriage is a universally available legal option. Stay abreast of these changes if you are opting out of legal marriage.

The logic of rescinding these statuses is that they were made available to couples who were unable to marry by law, but now that marriage is available as an option, couples should marry if they want to receive the rights and responsibilities that come with the marital status. Some entities claim that it is no longer necessary to bear the administrative burden of managing the additional statuses. Others have expressed a concern that they could be vulnerable to a suit by different-sex couples alleging discrimination if more relationship status options are available to same-sex couples but that they must marry to seek the same protections we can obtain by other means.

When corporations and municipalities phase out domestic partnership benefits, they force people to get married and, furthermore, to marry on someone else's timeline. This is unfortunate; many couples wish to retain the legal status they had enjoyed, such as the ability to enroll their partner in employer-provided health insurance, without the constraints of marriage.

Elimination of these other forms of relationship recognition is problematic not only for folks who choose not to marry but also for other family structures that benefit from these alternative benefits as well. I live in a community where many people build and organize families in more complex constellations than heterosexual nuclear families. All of these families are indeed *family*—and deserve recognition. In Miami, people with roots in the Caribbean, South America, and Central America constitute a majority. These are cultures that frequently live in cross-generational family structures where grandparents or aunts and uncles are primary caregivers. In addition to people living in stable nonmonogamous relationships, polyamorous couples or throuples (a committed relationship among three people, also known as a triad, a triple, or a trilationship) in long-term solid relationships deserve strong protections that recognize the relationship formations of their choosing. These are just a few of the many kinds of families who benefit from registries to provide needed protections. To phase out all other ways to recognize other kinds of familial relationships is to fail to recognize that two people (or more) can be emotionally and financially interdependent but that their relationship may not be able to fit into the law's rigid boxes.

Several jurisdictions have been struggling with how to treat these alternative statuses in light of the freedom to marry. The general assumption is that couples who are in civil unions or domestic partnerships must take the affirmative step of marrying each other to be considered legally married (rather than in a civil union or domestic partnership)—additional action should be required. Only in the states of Washington and Connecticut did state-registered domestic partnerships or civil unions automatically convert into marriages without any additional action by the couple. In every other jurisdiction with domestic partnership or civil union status before marriage equality, couples still needed to marry to receive the rights of marriage.

If you are marrying a partner with whom you have a domestic partnership or civil union, you need not dissolve it. In fact, having that additional status could give you closer to the full length of the committed relationship for support and other purposes. As the political and social realities of marriage equality were developing in the United States, many same-sex couples registered for every domestic partnership possible. They wanted to do whatever they could, whenever and wherever they could, to have their relationship legally recognized. There is no real need to undo those if you are staying together, marrying or not, unless you were in a domestic partnership with someone else and are now seeking to marry a different person, in which case you must dissolve that prior union rather than create a potential complication where you simultaneously have a legal status with two different people.

Alternatives to marriage statuses and recognitions vary by state and are changing each day. The best thing to do if you have questions is visit competent local counsel. You can also do some advance research prior to discussing your situation with an attorney at www.nclrights.org; there you will find, under the "Resources" tab, a marriage section with many publications available online for free, updated constantly as changes continue to unfold. Be sure that you provide the complete picture to your lawyer, naming each status you entered into so that a court can be specifically asked to dissolve each one.

7

TRANSGENDER AND MARRYING

When we lose the right to be different, we lose the privilege to be free.

—*Charles Evans Hughes*

If you are trans and about to marry, three particular issues could affect you. First, if you are trans and married, or if you are already married to someone who has transitioned, marriage equality resolved one worry that you might not have even known existed. Depending on where you live and whether you married before or after transitioning, the validity of your marriage might have been in question. If your state still refuses to recognize a change in gender marker, your marriage to someone of the same gender as your birth gender may have been considered invalid by those states. For example, Mark and Chris were living in Kansas and married there. They considered themselves married even though Chris was a trans woman. Kansas disregarded Chris's formal change of her name and gender marker, taking the position that DNA is what defines one's gender, which is therefore not modifiable. Prior to *Obergefell*, this situation created a real problem for couples, but because the Supreme Court of the United States made it crystal clear in *Obergefell* that all marriages between two persons, whether of the same sex or different sexes, are valid. All couples, including couples with a trans partner, are married. Note that transgender spouses may still encounter arguments about gender and validity of the marriage even after marriage equality. It is important to seek assistance from a competent attorney and an LGBT legal organization that has experience working on these cases.

Second, if you are trans and about to marry, consider having your spouse memorialize knowledge of your status. There have been some awful cases decided around the country, largely in the divorce context, wherein a cisgender (the "cis-" prefix refers to someone who is not transgender) spouse claims the marriage to a transgender person is a fraud because of misrepresentation or failure by the trans spouse to disclose her status. This situation seems preposterous—and it is—but if you identify as a different gender than you were assigned at birth, consider having a basic written understanding that your spouse is aware of that fact. As awkward and untrusting as it might feel to memorialize such an understanding, imagine how much worse it would be to have this discussion if custody of your children or ownership of shared property was placed in jeopardy as the issue of gender transition was litigated in front of a potentially hostile judge.

Finally, many transgender people wonder about name changes in conjunction with marriage. Surname changes can be done quite easily in concert with marriage, but if you are seeking to change your first name to reflect the gender with which you identify, you will want to handle that through the formal name change process, rather than via marriage. Marriage changes your last name (and possibly your middle name), not your first name. Moreover, when changing your first name, you will want to change your gender marker legally as well if that is what you want in your transition. In no case can the gender marker change be accomplished through marriage. When you have a court or administrative order that specifies a gender marker change, then the driver's license, passport, Social Security record, and other entities will fall into line. Many jurisdictions have a process through which you can obtain the forms through the local court system and handle the name and gender change yourself, without the assistance of an attorney, and some states have an administrative process for gender changes. It is wise, however, to have the assistance of counsel to ensure that the process, including the gender marker change, happens smoothly.

8
SOLVING PROBLEMS

Seldom or never does a marriage develop into an individual relationship smoothly and without crises. There is no birth of consciousness without pain.

—Carl Jung

All relationships are work. Marriage means that it is harder to just move out and move on. For the most part, that is a good thing. Ideally, your partner helps you grow and be a better you. The rewards of sticking with someone through thick and thin are substantial. Long-term couples often describe their commitment to the *process* of a marriage and not just a *person*. They embrace a mind-set of sticking to it and not bailing on the commitment made to this other soul. Of course, this ethos of endurance is inappropriate in the face of serious issues such as nonconsensual infidelity, substance abuse, or any form of domestic violence or abuse. Otherwise, the mentality of working it out is a worthwhile mind-set to adopt.

Sometimes, though, you need some help remembering what the heck you adored about your other half at the altar that day. When you want to hurl that soul into oncoming traffic, a refresher on what you were thinking when you committed is beneficial. It takes a village to nurture a marriage. All the people who witnessed your wedding—whether live or on social media—are your village. Turn to them for support. Straight marriages have long been buttressed by in-laws, friends, and broader religious and secular communities.

As we discussed in Chapter 3, one of the central purposes of inviting friends and family to a wedding is to ask them to remind you, when the going gets rough, of the depth of the love you have for your spouse.

COUNSELING

Friends and relatives are important, but sometimes you need a professional. Do not be afraid to reach out to a counselor. A few sessions often can get you back on track. It's important to remain vigilant about communication throughout the course of your marriage. Maintaining the connection with your spouse runs the risk of becoming less a priority as life gets in the way. This is particularly true for couples with children. A good therapist will help you sort out what is going on in your relationship. She or he can facilitate conflict resolution with your spouse, for example, reconciling different approaches to saving versus spending money, or finding ways to make each other feel loved, appreciated, and respected. You might have very different communication styles, and so you may hear something different from what he means. Having an unbiased mental health professional "translate" can be invaluable.

Oftentimes we replicate bad habits we learned from our parents or play "old tapes" from earlier in the relationship or prior relationships. Sometimes all options for conflict resolution have been exhausted and the relationship needs to end; that's okay. A therapist can help you come to that conclusion or, if you are there already, help you end the relationship in a way that is healthy for both of you. If there are children in the picture, a therapist can be especially important in keeping your eyes on the prize and fostering an environment less toxic than what often comes with divorce.

If what you want is to end the relationship and your spouse is not on the same page, couples counseling can help. Therapy can be just as useful in breaking up as in staying together. Someone who is not initially able to face that a relationship has run its course will be far more able to do so with the assistance of a neutral person to facilitate that conversation. No matter whether you live in a rural place, a major metropolitan area, or something in between, the LGBT community is a smallish town. It will serve you better not to burn a bridge if it is not an absolute necessity. Plus it is just plain toxic to have unnecessary drama. Try to work things out in a healthy way so that you can close a chapter of your life cordially and move on with minimal histrionics.

None of this will happen in a single therapy session. Commit to several sessions together, maybe three to five visits, and see where that takes you both. Examining our psyches—why we say what we say and do what we do—can be painful and messy work, but you will both undoubtedly come out on the other side better for it. In gaining self-understanding through the therapeutic process, you might also think about the psychological impact marriage itself has on what it feels like to be a person in a same-sex relationship.

Self-Understanding

MICHAEL ACTON-COLES

Therapist

Author, *Narcissism & Co-Dependency: Both Sides of the Coin*

London, England, and Miami, Florida

From a psychological standpoint, it is important to recognize that people who identify as LGBT, while united in their experience of discrimination, have experienced very different journeys in all other respects and arrive together at this pivotal point in history having formed attitudes and opinions as varied as those held by the heterosexual majority.

For some, the ability to form a legally sanctioned marriage is of psychological importance. It may help them to create a familial solidarity, perhaps enabling them to come to terms with the acceptance and security they may have lost after coming out to their parents and siblings and being rejected. The trauma will still be there, compounded in some sad cases by the effects of homelessness, but the ability to create their own family unit, founded on love, equality, and mutual respect, will often help them to rebuild their shattered sense of belonging.

But many couples, both heterosexual and homosexual, see no need to sanctify their relationships with marriage vows, and this is the first time that LGBT couples will have had to assess their attitude toward marriage. For some, this will lead to a painful parting of the ways, either before the wedding ceremony or afterward, as they realize they do not share each other's visions, hopes, or beliefs.

Same-sex marriage is not just a question for those who are heterosexual or Bible-thumpers or anti-gay; it also touches on our own internalized phobias. It may be okay if we want to live together and spend the rest of our lives with each other, but saying vows might provoke something in us that causes us to start opening up questions about being gay, our religious convictions, personal beliefs, and the like.

For example, if you are Catholic, you cannot get married in a Catholic church. While the law has said it is okay, what about our churches and our belief systems? Are the legal changes paying mere lip service to what we really want? If heterosexuals get married in a Catholic church, they have mandatory pre-marriage courses; in Judaism it is the same. Because the churches, for the most part, are not supporting the legal changes, gay couples do not have access to those premarital courses, which can be beneficial. In any case, many LGBT people have dispensed with the church a long time ago. (When an institution tells you that your behavior is unnatural and sinful this is not surprising!) To them, the idea that they are now expected to conform to stereotypes they see as oppressive and an attack against personal and sexual freedom is unwelcome. Their views have given rise to the vocal protest group Gays Against Gay Marriage. What is clear is that the legal changes afford opportunity and equality along with confusion and individual challenge.

A therapist would be well advised to develop a pre-marriage course to help address these concerns. I personally mediate such issues during an agreed solution-focused therapeutic contract, usually lasting approximately six weeks. It may be a good idea for those considering marriage to attend a few sessions with a therapist to go through what it means for them, what their expectations are, and, if their expectations are reasonable and the marriage does happen, how they would decide things such as who would work more and who would work less, what happens to their joint cars, what happens to their contributions, how the couple will handle guests who cause trouble or are too controlling—all of the things that heterosexuals go through.

A therapist used to working with families and couples can use breadth of experience to truly explore the positive and negative ways the marriage is likely to impact their relationship. The positives might include deeper commitment and a nice celebration, but on the flip side there could be negatives such as not being able to just step out the way you used to. Does marriage mean monogamy or is there going to be an open relationship? Are some of the standards for gay relationships going to transcend marriage? There may be a dual agenda: one partner may be thinking that when they get married, they can continue as they have been, and the other might be thinking that in the eyes of their religion or belief system a marriage is a marriage. There are also issues around the custody of children and pets, not to mention all the monetary issues. Prenups and postnups are important, and if you have not gotten a prenup, you might want to think about a postnup.

We must not forget that, as a result of social conditioning, there may be psychological issues around public displays of affection. While one member of a couple may see a wedding ceremony as a long overdue opportunity to display her affection and commitment openly, the other may feel anxious, or even horrified, at the thought of kissing or even holding hands in the glare of the outside world. The internal homophobia that results from years of being told that homosexuality is "disgusting" and "unnatural" cannot simply be swept away with a change in the law, and many LGBT people admit to feeling uncomfortable and even repulsed by seeing gay couples openly indulging in such displays. The media focus that has put gay marriage under the spotlight has also galvanized elements of those opposed to the movement, leaving couples vulnerable to—and anxious about—public hostility, or even hostility from one of the fiancés on their special day, stemming from his awkwardness or embarrassment.

For those couples who do decide to marry, a steep learning curve awaits on both the psychological and legal levels. It must be understood that, growing up, LGBT people have always lacked the relationship templates that heterosexuals take for granted. Few box office hits, TV shows, press articles, and family or social gatherings demonstrate the existence of wholesome and loving same-sex couples. In fact, we learn quite the opposite—to fear our attraction and feelings—and are often negatively impacted as a result. Rejection from society can have profound effects on self-esteem, which in turn can harm career prospects and, with that, the ability to provide for a family. Consequently, it is a sad fact that many LGBT individuals are employed in positions far below their capability, which is reported to create a significant predisposition toward forming an unhealthy codependent relationship.

The concept of a wedding is that we have our nearest and dearest there to give us a way to celebrate with us. In a same-sex marriage, that's not always the case, and this can inflame any existing unease. The happy events of extended families—births, weddings, housewarmings, and so on—can be a source of pain for LGBT people if they are excluded from their spouse's wider circle or if their spouse is introduced as a "friend."

Despite all of the challenges above, the legalization of same-sex marriage has given those who do take their vows a voice, and that voice will only grow clearer and more confident as LGBT couples, and society in general, become more accustomed to what this new institution means. There are around fifteen hundred rights and obligations that affect newly married couples, covering everything from child custody and property inheritance to next-of-kin status and tax reporting; that's a lot to learn and become comfortable with, particularly when you know that many states will be adjusting to the changes, too—some less willingly than others. Also, lest we forget, money, children, and property can be used as weapons when a marriage is breaking down, and especially so when this happens in a legal arena. Now, more therapeutic mediation will be required before and after the wedding if a same-sex couple is going to navigate this new territory.

One very topical issue at the moment is domestic abuse, and when the U.S. Supreme Court granted the freedom to marry, all states would have to recognize not only that LGBT marriages exist but also that the rule of law applies equally to them. Domestic abuse in the LGBT population is at least as prevalent as it is in the heterosexual population, and possibly more widespread. The legalization of gay marriage will help to provide a platform for abused spouses to speak out about their situation; we can only hope that this will encourage those who are not married but are suffering abuse to follow suit. In addition, it makes it more likely that funding will be found to provide therapeutic help and safe houses to victims of domestic violence.

So while the legalization of marriage has undoubtedly brought hope to many people identifying as LGBT, the inner psychological battle for freedom, equality, and understanding goes on.

MEDIATION

If you have spent some time with a couples counselor working on relationship issues but still cannot resolve your conflict, consider turning to a mediator. A mediator is specifically trained in conflict resolution and will focus on helping the two of you come up with solutions together. Similar to working with a couples therapist, a mediator gives you both a neutral perspective on your relationship. Mediators are often lawyers, even retired judges, but they can be therapists or anyone (licensed, of course) with a knack for assisting people with problem solving. Some mediators are especially certified in family matters, and some of those mediators have substantial experience working with same-sex couples. If one of these specialists is in your community, he or she could be a good place to start, to ensure a certain level of comfort and competence.

Mediators do not listen to both sides and pronounce a decision; that is what an arbitrator does. An arbitrator is typically a retired judge who does issue binding decisions, which, like it or not, you have to live with. Rather, a mediator works with you both (either in one room together or in "caucus," where the spouses are in separate rooms, with or without lawyers, and the mediator goes back and forth) to bring about a compromise.

I am a licensed family mediator. I have sat down with many couples to help them resolve their relationship conflicts. Unfortunately, usually by the time they come to me for mediation, they are breaking up. I find myself often wishing they had come to me or a therapist before communication deteriorated so badly. If your relationship is on the skids, do not wait until you have said and done things you cannot take back. Act prophylactically. It is possible an agreement about the conflict can be hammered out, whether written or oral, and the relationship can continue to move forward and flourish.

Being deliberate at the beginning of your relationship and addressing problems early is crucial. This work is not spontaneous or fun, but its reward is less drama down the line.

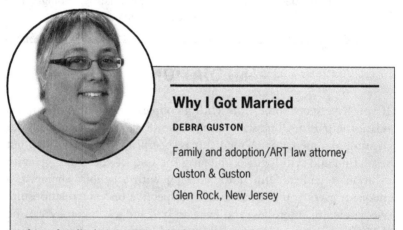

Why I Got Married

DEBRA GUSTON

Family and adoption/ART law attorney

Guston & Guston

Glen Rock, New Jersey

As a family law attorney in New Jersey for almost twenty-eight years, I have heard a lot of stories about how and why my straight clients get married. Most love each other; some marry for the sake of a child they did not plan; others marry to please their families; and every once in a while there is a drunken trip to the altar. There are weddings in backyards, on deserted islands, and in musty churches.

But many of my gay and lesbian clients have told me that they married because, well, they could, and there was a party sponsored by a statewide LGBT advocacy group. That's it—it was fun, it was political, and everyone else was doing it. I have also dealt with divorces where one of the spouses tries to argue away a marital obligation because he just went along with the crowd and had no idea what he was getting into—nobody told him the fun came with strings attached. And, wow, it was so easy to get into; how come it is so hard to get out of?

Our state's journey to marriage equality is probably not different from many, but our experience of same-sex couples' options for legal relationships has been expansive. When domestic partnerships became available at the beginning of July 2004, the political groups got a bunch of municipal registrars to open the town halls on Saturday, and *everyone* who was *anyone* became domestic partners in celebration of Independence Day. Three years later, civil unions came into being on President's Day. Again, parties ensued, municipal employees got holiday pay, and dozens of gay folks got "civil unioned." What a great way to celebrate the birthdays of two of our greatest presidents! Marriage came to New Jersey on an inauspicious day in October, 2013—but do not think there were not dozens of weddings performed en masse at the stroke of midnight on October 21, 2013, presided over by a U.S. senator and lots of progressive mayors.

"Mom, Dad, I eloped to the rally on Saturday in the next town over—the executive director of a political group spoke and wished us and a hundred other couples a hearty *mazel tov!*"

9
ESTATE PLANNING

He who fails to plan is planning to fail.

—Winston Churchill

Regardless of whether they marry, *all* couples should take steps to protect each other and themselves. If you decide not to marry, estate planning is of even greater importance; you will not have automatic inheritance rights or have the presumptive ability to make medical decisions in the event your partner cannot communicate. These rights are important and among the reasons why we have been fighting for marriage. Ensure that you secure these essential rights through comprehensive estate planning for your partner—or another designee.

The basic elements of an estate plan are:

- *Will:* A will is a simple way to direct what you want to happen to your stuff at the time of your death. In a will, you specify a personal representative to administer your estate through the probate process and, if you have children, whom you wish to be the guardian of any minor children. Even if you do not have much money or own any real estate, having a will is important.

- *Durable power of attorney:* Durable power of attorney gives your partner the power to do almost everything on your behalf. These powers are effective immediately in many states and are very serious, giving your designee complete authority over your financial affairs upon execution.

- *Designation of health care surrogate:* Known by various names in different states, a designated health care proxy grants access and decision making in the health care context. Health care providers love this document because they know whom they can turn to for consent if you cannot direct them yourself.

- *Living will:* If you develop a terminal condition, an advance medical directive states your intention for how you would want to be treated and in what cases you would want various treatments or heroic measures utilized to keep you alive.

- *Designation of pre-need guardian:* Should a court determine you legally incapacitated and unable to handle your medical and financial decisions, a guardian may be appointed. Specify whom you would want to serve as guardian, or the court will appoint someone else.

- *Designation of pre-need guardian for minor child:* If you have a minor child, many states allow you to designate a guardian to care for him or her in the event of your disability. Along with a second-parent adoption, this is helpful to be sure that the next person in line is given authority to care for your child if you or your other legal co-parent are not able to.

Married couples still need an estate plan. Do not assume that you do not need estate planning documents simply because you live in a jurisdiction that recognizes your marriage. Only twenty-one countries worldwide recognize marriage equality. If you find yourself somewhere that does not recognize all marriages, you may be legal strangers to each other. We are a mobile society, and until there is both worldwide marriage recognition and zero risk of encountering homophobic or ill-informed authorities, it is critical to take the belt-and-suspenders approach—that is, extra precautionary measures. Let's say you are on the trip of a lifetime in Australia, currently the only developed English-speaking country that does not allow same-sex couples to marry. Your spouse has a hiking accident and gets rushed to the local hospital. You are not allowed in the ambulance. No one gives you information about his condition and treatment at the hospital. In this moment of crisis, you do not want to have to devote your attention to a possibly futile argument that this is your husband; you will just want to be by your beloved's bedside. Do not add anxiety to that stressful medical emergency. Have a few simple pieces of paper with you: a power of attorney, a living will, and designations of health care surrogate and pre-need guardian. While there is no guarantee that these documents will be respected each and every place you travel, it is far better to have them than not. They do not take up a lot of space in your luggage and cost a relatively small amount of money to have drawn up by a reputable attorney.

Every single person, gay or straight, single or coupled, married or unmarried, needs an estate plan. Often when I mention estate planning, people dismiss the suggestion. They claim that they do not have enough assets for an estate. They are mistaken. An estate does not have to be big. An estate simply may be your modest bank account and your personal property, including your car, jewelry, household items, clothing, and pets.

Yes, pets. I had a case back in 2000 where a television photojournalist died in a helicopter crash on the job. He and his partner of four years were planning to celebrate their commitment to each other by drawing up their wills and health care documents. Unfortunately, they did not finish that project before the terrible accident. In the absence of an estate plan, the family of the deceased partner swooped in and took everything, including the couple's dog. The family's lawyer actually asked, at mediation, whether we had a receipt for the dog to prove that my client was entitled to keep him. An estate plan would have provided an easier path to justice for my grieving client, who was left homeless. An estate plan makes your intentions clear.

WILL

The most essential part of any estate plan is a last will and testament, known colloquially as a will. A will directs someone, whom attorneys call your executor or personal representative, how to handle your stuff upon your death. If you do not have a will, everything you own in your name alone will transfer according to your state's laws of intestacy ("intestacy" means dying without a will). State law usually directs inheritance to follow a certain order: legally wedded spouse, children, parents, siblings, grandparents, and then descendants of grandparents. Notice that nowhere on that list is your boyfriend or girlfriend.

A will designates an executor, or personal representative, who handles the administration of your estate. If you are not married, your executor is the person named in your will. If you do not have a will, the person who will be appointed by the court will likely be the same person who will inherit from you pursuant to the laws of intestacy. Years ago I had a client whose partner died. Since their assets were owned jointly, they thought they did not need wills. Alas, the parent of the partner who passed away got herself appointed personal representative and fought the surviving partner for every little item of personal property, from the music collection to their tools. It was both absurd and terribly painful for the grieving survivor to engage in that battle.

In forty states, marriage can result in your spouse having automatic inheritance rights upon death, no matter what your estate plan says. A spouse might have a right to take anywhere from a third to a half of your estate even if she was not provided for in your estate plan. If you are fine with that, great; if not, you need a written nuptial agreement to the contrary.

There are many kinds of revocable and irrevocable trusts. Trust planning, particularly for higher-net-worth folks, can be an important strategy for preserving assets during disability or at death. A few types of trust vehicles are available only to married couples. Regardless of marital status, trusts are useful vehicles for people who want to restrict a beneficiary's access to the trust corpus—for example, children too young to inherit the bulk of an estate. If you want to provide your significant other or spouse with funds for her life but then at her death you want those funds to revert to, for example, your birth family, your child, or a charity, a trust is the logical way to accomplish that goal.

Titling your assets in the name of a trust avoids the probate process. Probate is a court-supervised way to pass property held in the sole name of a decedent to her beneficiaries as named in her will or, if there is no will, by the laws of intestacy. Probate filings are a matter of public record. In some states probate can be costly and cause substantial delay in the distribution of assets to intended beneficiaries. Property owned by a trust passes outside probate. Rather than someone having to serve as an executor or administrator, the successor trustee handles easily the transfer of assets. Usually, paying an attorney to set up a trust costs more than a will, but for some families it is well worth it.

Another reason to have testamentary documents in place is to provide for what happens to your property at the death of the second partner. If your partner survives you and she inherits everything you have worked hard to accumulate, all of that property will pass to her family or designated beneficiaries at her death if you do not coordinate your estate plans. As a couple, you might want to provide for other family members or a charity. Consider taking the opportunity to support worthy not-for-profit organizations that do good work in the community. You will leave a nice legacy and get a swell tax deduction to boot.

Jackie and Lisa's Story
••••••••••

Let's return to Jackie and Lisa. Jackie's intention was for her children to inherit everything from her at her death. Instead, since Jackie had no estate plan and was married, Lisa inherited fully half of Jackie's estate, contrary to what Jackie had hoped. Imagine that a year after Jackie dies, Lisa dies. Lisa does not have an estate plan either, and all of her assets pass to her sister, as Lisa's surviving next of kin. If Lisa had an estate plan benefiting Jackie's children, Jackie's children could have received what their mom wanted them to have, including all of the assets their mom built up, such as investment accounts and the house. Otherwise, Jackie's assets would pass to Lisa's family. In fact, Jackie and Lisa could have done an estate plan together, saying that their assets would pass to each other at death and then, at the death of the second to die, could go half to Jackie's family and half to Lisa's family. Of course, Jackie would have had to trust that Lisa wouldn't change her will after Jackie's death, which she easily could have done, as wills are totally revocable. Among other solutions, Jackie might have considered putting a trust in place saying that her children were the beneficiaries either at her death or, if she wanted Lisa to have access to funds for her life, then at Lisa's death.

DURABLE POWER OF ATTORNEY

A durable power of attorney delegates financial powers. The most serious of all the documents that you sign in the estate planning process, a durable power of attorney is the instrument through which you authorize another person to handle your financial affairs, including signing checks, conveying property, and a host of other extraordinarily significant powers. Many states require that these documents be effective upon signature rather than upon proof of incapacity at some future time.

Some people are nervous at the thought of granting someone this power, so they suggest executing these documents only when needed. It is possible, though, that circumstances may make it impossible to get a document signed, witnessed, and notarized when it is actually needed. You might get in an accident, be involuntarily hospitalized, or be traveling and need your attorney-in-fact (that is the name for the agent appointed in the durable power of attorney) to jump into action.

The attorney-in-fact is in a fiduciary relationship to you, which means that there is a standard of care required; if that standard is breached, he or she is liable for damages. No one wants to sue, so delegate this power to someone you trust implicitly. If you have a durable power of attorney in place and the relationship sours, whether because of an acrimonious breakup or because you no longer have that level of trust in the person you designated, revoke the power with a simple written statement saying that the document is no longer effective, and deliver your statement to any banks or other institutions that you gave it to so that they know they can no longer rely upon it.

The "durable" part of the power of attorney means that the decision and assignation survives your incapacity (a disability or impairment whereupon you cannot be responsible for making competent decisions). The document remains effective when you most need someone to handle your financial affairs. The vast majority of the powers typically granted in these documents are not automatically granted to married couples. Do not be lulled into a sense of complacency, thinking that marriage obviates the need for a durable power of attorney. When discussing the provisions of durable powers of attorney with clients, I am sometimes told that they have often signed their spouse's name anyway, not realizing or caring they were not legally permitted to do that in the absence of specific authority. While you might get away with signing your sweetie's name or pretending to be her on the phone sometimes, you do want to have a durable power of attorney in place in case you are ever challenged about your authority to act on her behalf.

ADVANCE DIRECTIVES

Advance directives include living wills, health care proxies, and guardianship designations. Advance directives are essential for everyone, in case the unexpected happens. Each document is important. Anyone and everyone, gay or straight, single or coupled, married or unmarried, should have these documents in place.

- A *living will* outlines your wishes for end-of-life care. Usually a one- or two-page document, a living will states under what circumstances you want to be kept alive by heroic measures. A living will is only effective at the very end of life, when there is no reasonable hope for recovery. It is your authorization for the treating physician to consult with your designee regarding whether to continue life-prolonging treatment. Depending on your stated wishes, your health care provider is empowered to remove artificial means of keeping you alive, should you be in a persistent vegetative state, an end-stage condition, or the final stages of a terminal illness. If you have specific preferences for the end of life, such as not wanting to be intubated, indicate them in a living will. If you think that once you are married you do not need to have a living will, you are wrong. Recall the case of Terri Schiavo. Schiavo's husband and parents spent the better part of fifteen years arguing with each other through the courts, the legislature, and various public forums about removing the feeding tube keeping her alive when she was in a persistent vegetative state. Her husband alleged that she would not have wanted to be kept alive given the slim chances for recovery; her parents felt otherwise. Had Terri Schiavo had a simple living will specifically stating both her wishes regarding life support and that she wanted her husband to have the ultimate authority to make the call about removing treatment based on doctor's recommendations, she would have been able to rest in peace years earlier.

- A *designation of health care surrogate*, known variously as a health care proxy or power of attorney for health care, names a preferred person(s) to have access to you and make medical decisions for you in the event you cannot communicate or decide for yourself. This document needs to be crystal clear about what powers you want your beloved or other designee to have. For example, the Health Insurance Portability and Accountability Act (HIPAA) is the privacy act, which you will want to be sure you waive, in writing, with respect to your partner/spouse. HIPAA is variously used as a weapon and a shield with regard to patient information. "Privacy concerns" can sometimes be the excuse that a health care provider will give when she does not want to deal with you, your questions, and even your gayness. HIPAA can even be invoked to cut off conversation when you are simply trying to relay information about your partner's medical history, allergies, and the like. A HIPAA release is not automatic for married couples, and HIPAA release language is helpful for health care providers to see so that they know they cannot withhold any of your medical information from your spouse. Whether the HIPAA waiver is a separate document or incorporated into this advance directive, be sure it is in place. Just like a durable power of attorney and a living will, the authority of the health care surrogate expires when you do. Some attorneys therefore prefer to have a HIPAA release executed separately from the designation of health care surrogate in case there is a need to obtain medical records after death, for example to pursue a medical malpractice claim.

- A *designation of pre-need guardian* names someone to manage your affairs if you should become legally incapacitated over a longer term (such as from Alzheimer's, a coma, or other impairment). Sometimes that legal incapacity will induce a court to want to institute a guardianship or a conservatorship in order to supervise your care and the administration of your assets. A guardianship is never ideal in that it is intrusive and the filings, including an annual inventory of your assets and liabilities, are a matter of public record. But should a guardianship need to be put in place, the court will look to what you put in writing when it appoints a guardian. Your estate plan should include a document that names someone to serve in that capacity.

Parents need additional documents in their estate plans. If you have a child and are co-parenting with someone who is not that child's legal parent, pursue a second-parent adoption if possible. As discussed in the section "Moms and Moms, Dads and Dads" in Chapter 4, second-parent adoptions protect the parental rights of the nonlegal parent through a simple adoption process. Even if her name appears on the birth certificate of the child, every nonbiological parent should have some sort of court order confirming parental rights. Be sure to have a *designation of pre-need guardian for minor child*, or its equivalent, in place as well as a statement in your will that you wish for your partner to be the child's legal guardian. A will kicks in when you die; the pre-need designation is effective in the event that you become legally incapacitated (meaning a court determines that you are not competent to function as a parent). If either happens, naming your partner as the child's legal guardian is crucial evidence to help a court determine what is in the best interests of the child. If there is another legal parent (such as an ex-husband), these provisions are not likely to be binding statements, but certainly the likelihood of your intentions being respected on some level is markedly greater if put in writing in your estate plan.

For all of these documents, you will want to be sure not only that your beloved is named, but also that you have an alternate listed as well in case the primary person is unable to serve, such as if you and your partner are in an accident together. List the name, current phone numbers, email address, and street address for all designees so that they can be reached promptly in an emergency. Do not forget to review these documents every year or two to be sure that the contact information is up to date. You do not want a health care provider trying to reach you on your old cell phone.

Pay attention to the specific execution requirements of your state. You do not want to end up with documents that are not worth the paper they are printed on. A competent lawyer, licensed where you live, can make a difference in the effectiveness of your plans. Do not cut corners using an inexpensive online document assembly service. These often do not provide you with documents conforming to your individual state laws. Since we are more on the move than ever, I tend to be on the safe side and use witnesses and notaries a bit more than my state might require, just to give the document added chance of being honored where execution requirements may differ.

STORING AND RETRIEVING THE DOCUMENTS

Lawyers' personal practices vary in whether we hold on to originals in our offices. There is not a single right way to handle this. When I assist clients in preparing these documents, we create two sets of originals: one that we retain in my office for safekeeping, and another that we provide to the client along with a few copies that we suggest be given to the primary designee, the alternate designee, and the most-visited physician. Each document prominently says that a copy of the document is as effective as the original. This clear direction to a health care provider or other authority can save time and heartache if you are being pressed to provide an original. I advise against keeping your estate planning documents in a safe deposit box. Too often that practice results in an inability to access the documents at the time they are most needed. Keep them in a safe place at home that is logical, such as a desk drawer or file cabinet, should someone need to look for them. The documents are only useful if available when needed.

Another tool to consider having in your arsenal, whether you are married or unmarried, is a 24/7 way to retrieve these advance directives in case the unexpected happens and you do not have the physical documents with you. There are companies such as DocuBank, Legal Vault, and others that provide access affordably and immediately. When you enroll in such a service, your advance directives are scanned and emailed to them. You receive a card with a personal identification number (PIN). You keep that card in your wallet adjacent to your health insurance card, since that is where a health care provider is going to be looking for a source of payment. If you are awake and aware when being admitted and do not have your advance directives on hand, you would direct the provider to that card. She can access a website or toll-free number and input the PIN number to instantaneously receive your documents anywhere in the world. If you are zonked out for whatever reason, a health care provider could find the card and act. Name and contact information for your next of kin and your doctor are printed on the card, so that they can be contacted in case of emergency. The card can list any allergies or medical conditions that you have, which can be life-saving information to have in a crisis moment.

Folks often show me their own free versions of this concept, which might include a USB drive or some cloud-based access. Those are better than nothing, but there can be an added sense of credibility given to documents forwarded directly to the health care provider by a third party, not to mention that you might not be conscious and able to provide access to the cloud-based information or have the jump drive with you. Sometimes even a delay of a few minutes can mean disaster.

Estate planning remains of vital importance to our community. Do not be lulled into thinking that marriage equality means either that we will be treated fairly the world over or that homophobia is a thing of the past. Sometimes health care providers are not prejudiced, but they are just not aware of changes in the law. Other times they may be fully aware but use ignorance as a pretext to make your life more difficult. For those reasons as well as clarity of intention, get your ducks in a row. Like the now less homophobic Boy Scouts say, "be prepared."

10
NUPTIAL AGREEMENTS

First, drawing up a prenuptial agreement together is a sign
of incredible trust and financial openness—you're fooling
yourself if you think you can achieve complete intimacy
without it.

—*Suze Orman*

I f your fairy-tale marriage should turn into a horror story, your
union will be subject to the same laws and procedures of divorce
as heterosexual marriage, for better or worse. Marriage stipulates
certain defaults upon death or divorce. If you wish to modify those
defaults, consider what is known as a premarital or prenuptial agreement. A prenup is an agreement that is entered into before marriage
and sets out what would happen to your assets and liabilities and lays
out any spousal support obligations or waivers if you divorce or if
you die while married. A prenup can help you live somewhat happily ever after.

As challenging as it can be to contemplate the potential end to a
marriage just as you are getting into it, think of it less as evidence
of negativity and more as a demonstration of maturity. Between 30
and 50 percent of all marriages end in divorce. If you knew you had
a 30 percent chance of being in a car accident or losing your home in
a fire, would you not get car insurance or homeowner's insurance?
Be realistic: your marriage could be among them, and it is better to
choose your own exit terms while the two of you are getting along

than subject yourself to the arbitrary and ever-changing laws of the state that will govern you in the event of a divorce without a prenuptial agreement. Generally, assets are divided equally upon divorce. That might be perfectly fine in your situation. If you have a situation that is outside the norm (like Tania, whose family wants to protect her interest in the bodega they own, or Jackie, who has kids from a prior marriage), you would want to consider having an agreement like this in place.

WHO NEEDS A PRENUP?

Without a prenup, you might have to hand over half of your assets at a divorce. You may lose a portion of the value of assets and accounts you brought into the marriage or inherited during the marriage based on how you treated those assets during the marriage. You could be on the hook for alimony (also called spousal support or spousal maintenance). Your spouse could have automatic rights to inherit from you in an amount greater than you intend, unless there is an agreement waiving those rights to your estate. If you are concerned about protecting your assets and not assuming debts that you did not personally incur, you may need a prenup.

On the flip side, if you are the spouse with fewer assets, you might have different concerns that a prenup can address. If you feel you would need to be provided with a roof over your head, receive spousal support, or have your attorney's fees paid upon divorce, know that you could be denied that if the marriage is of a shorter term, your spouse has better lawyers, or a judge does not deem it equitable. If your legal marriage happened many years into your committed relationship and you split after just a few years of being legally married, you could be treated unfairly in the divorce proceedings. There is no "credit for time served" in the relationship that precedes the commencement of the marital one.

Perhaps you are cool with having all of your assets and debts accumulated during the marriage divided equally should you divorce, in which case you may want a simple prenup that says so, to prevent someone waging an expensive legal battle to claim she is entitled to more than half of the assets. People who need to think seriously about prenups include those in situations where one or both partners have debt, kids, or a family business. If there is a big disparity in income and assets and if the possibility of having to give up half of your marital assets would be a problem, you would be wise to explore a prenup. If you are going to be the stay-at-home spouse and not work, you might want to be sure that there are provisions in place to make certain you would exit with certain assets and alimony, which can also be handled in a prenup.

For those who have been burned by a bad split in the past or witnessed that of a friend or relative, no amount of assurance provided by a prenuptial or a postnuptial agreement helps. Even when advised how to minimize conflict, including keeping income and assets separate, for some there is no way they would consider marrying, given the awfulness they have seen. I have heard quite a few people say they have never seen a marriage end well. These wounded souls often just prefer to avoid the whole institution of marriage and not take chances.

However, for those who want to take the marriage plunge with some protections in place regarding how assets, income, and debts would be handled in case of a divorce, a clearly written agreement prepared by a lawyer experienced with this kind of work can create great peace of mind. Promises can be made and broken, whether of the "I'll always take care of you, baby" or the "I would never go after something that was not mine" variety. These agreements can be entered into before the marriage, which is good timing, in order to make clear what everyone's expectations are before it is too late. The point of the agreement is to save the time and attorneys' fees associated with an adversarial divorce should the relationship end. Many people do not realize that overburdened court systems can tie couples up in divorce court for years while the monies they are battling over are being consumed by the professional fees.

If you are already married and realize that such an agreement would be prudent, a postnuptial agreement is an option. A postnup works the same way as a prenuptial agreement and has all the same provisions. It is just negotiated and executed *after* the marriage is solemnized. In many states, they are still as effective and enforceable, but be sure to check your state's law first. Explore a postnup to memorialize changing conditions in the marriage, such as if you are making a move for one person's career that means the other spouse's is disadvantaged.

TALKING ABOUT PRE- AND POSTNUPTIAL AGREEMENTS

The toughest aspect about these agreements may be how and when to discuss them. The ideal time is when both parties are on the same page and it is mutually understood that such an agreement is in everyone's best interests.

How old you are and how long you have been together prior to marrying can affect how difficult this conversation is to have. If you are two young people who have yet to accumulate much by way of assets, you might have a harder time justifying a belief that what you build up together in your (hopefully) long futures as a committed couple should remain separate. It may be different if you are getting married as an older person who has had many years of accumulating assets individually prior to the marriage. If your relationship dates back years or even decades before the legal marriage, a prenup might feel unfair if the assets you accumulated together are titled, for whatever reason, in the name of one partner as opposed to jointly. An agreement to maintain separate premarital property could read like codifying an unfair arrangement.

I often tell my clients to blame me and say their lawyer insisted on having a prenuptial agreement in place. I'm happy to take one for the team! Heck, I do not need to go to sleep and wake up with your soon-to-be spouse; I do not need to win a popularity contest. Many of us in the legal profession strongly encourage our clients to have a prenuptial agreement in place to manage everyone's expectations going into the marriage. Spending a little on a nuptial agreement can save our clients many thousands, tens of thousands, or even hundreds of thousands in an adversarial divorce. Ethical lawyers mention the prudence of putting an agreement in place even when it is an uncomfortable conversation.

Sometimes one's family of origin insists on the agreement in order to keep an inheritance or family business intact for future generations. That can be a blessing, in that it takes it out of your hands and you can pass the blame, or it can be a curse, making a nice family relationship awkward.

No matter what, having the candid conversation about prenuptial agreements is the mature thing to do. Do not wimp out!

MAKE SURE YOUR PRENUP HOLDS UP

Whether the agreement is pre- or postnuptial, keep in mind these two tips to increase the chances that this document is actually enforced. First, retain an attorney experienced in handling these agreements. There are state-specific requirements with regard to financial disclosure and terms that must be included and others that cannot be included. Second, resist the temptation to save money and use an agreement you find online or to modify the one your college roommate used for his marriage. Odds are those agreements will cost you more in the end. The consequences of an unenforceable agreement can be tremendous.

Challenges to these agreements arise during a divorce proceeding when one party is not happy with what was previously negotiated. Those challenges can result in the agreement being set aside, particularly if there are elements surrounding its execution that make it vulnerable to attack. Be sure that you have made honest and complete financial disclosure to each other, including listing all assets and debts. Each party should know what she is gaining and giving up by signing the agreement. Do not conceal anything, no matter how small the account or whether it is in another country: if you have any interest in it, list it. You would never want to face a challenge to the agreement down the road based on the argument that there was not full information divulged and that the agreement would not have been signed in the first place if that item had been disclosed.

If you are planning a prenup, be sure there is ample time before the wedding to avoid claims of duress. One of the common arguments made when trying to set aside a prenuptial agreement is that the agreement was concluded such a short time before the marriage that there was pressure to get it signed without negotiating the terms further. Unless your state has specific laws on the timing, there is no hard-and-fast guidance about how long one should wait between signing a prenup and the wedding ceremony. A good rule of thumb is at least two weeks. When I am contacted on Thursday by someone getting married on Sunday (which happens with alarming frequency), I suggest that she do a postnuptial agreement instead to avoid allegations that the parties were rushed. You do not want your partner to contend later that there was not reasoned consideration of the terms before the marriage. Generally each partner should have separate counsel. In fact, some states require it, especially if waiving support or other default protections of marriage. Having two lawyers seems counterintuitive to a loving couple in the glow of connubial bliss. If there is general agreement about the pre- or postnup, a couple might have a lawyer serve as a neutral party to prepare the agreement and then have another lawyer do a brief review to advise each party about the agreement's consequences from your sole perspective. Even if the whole process is amicable, it is a good idea to have each party represented by a lawyer only looking out for her own interests. Avoid the argument later that your ex, feeling jilted and wanting a better settlement walking out the door, was not properly counseled before signing the prenup and thus did not know what he was agreeing to.

Even if all of these execution tips are followed, your spouse might attempt to claim that the terms of a pre- or postnuptial agreement are sufficiently lopsided as to be unreasonable. That might be enough for it to be ruled unenforceable. Courts are generally not comfortable with an agreement that is terribly unfair or one-sided and they can set aside a contract as "unconscionable." For example, couples have all kinds of arrangements including where one spouse works outside the home and the other works inside the home, managing the domestic sphere. Kids or no kids, running a household is a lot of work. The law might refer to the stay-at-home spouse as the "impecunious spouse" and seek to be sure he was not taken advantage of in the agreement negotiations and is adequately provided for upon divorce. To live in such an arrangement but then to have a nuptial agreement in which the impecunious spouse waives all alimony, has to pay his own attorney's fees, and gets no assets whatsoever on divorce could be viewed as outrageous by a judge when asked to decide on the agreement's fairness.

Devising an equitable agreement is one way to avoid this outcome. A helpful aspect of entering into a nuptial agreement when you are happy and getting along is that it is easier to conceive of what would be fair to both parties. Once divorce is on the table, people sometimes develop convenient memory loss about what had worked for them when times were good. If you are a part of a relationship that has a substantial income, asset, or career disparity, apply what is known as the "sleep test" during agreement negotiations. Contemplate the deal that your spouse would get upon a split and make sure you could sleep at night if that were the ultimate outcome. Resist the temptation to think about what the law might allow you to get away with; rather, consider whether you would be able to put your head down on your pillow at peace with that result.

If you are the impecunious spouse, do not let your contributions to the home be devalued. An agreement that would create an unjust result for you should be approached with serious caution. A promise from your honey that she will revisit this agreement once you are together for a certain number of years should be memorialized in writing. These agreements can have built-in "expiration dates" if you draft them that way; do not trust an oral understanding. Do not be afraid to negotiate the terms, and do not accept the first draft presented to you in the hopes that it will all be over sooner that way. Push back. Get an agreement that represents a fair deal for all the hard work you do to keep the home running smoothly.

No matter what, do not be shy about discussing such conflicts. If you have a bad split and end up suffering substantial negative and preventable consequences, you might be sorry that you chose temporary peace of mind, fearing confrontation. Better to do it and do it right. With any luck, the preparation, negotiation, and execution of your nuptial agreement will be a colossal waste of time and money, because it will never be needed.

ELEMENTS OF PRE- AND POSTNUPTIAL AGREEMENTS

Pre- and postnuptial agreements are not one-size-fits-all documents. You can include almost anything that you agree upon now and want to avoid having a fight about later, with the exception of how child custody or visitation (called time-sharing in some states) and child support would be handled if you have children together. That is one thing not to include, as such agreements about children are not enforceable. The court's decision is always going to aim for the best interests of the child at the time of dissolution. Otherwise, premarital agreements are wide open to possibility.

Alimony

Pre- and postnuptial agreements can provide for spousal support or, in many states, waive it entirely. They can provide for different amounts of support payments, which increase in tiers over the duration of the marriage. There are different types of alimony. A prenup could, for example, include a waiver of permanent alimony (which would be paid until the death or remarriage of the payee spouse) in favor of a lump sum or payments for a specific period of years. Some states have a formula in which the length of time alimony is paid is based on the duration of the marriage, such as for one-third of the years of the marriage. That would mean that if you were married for twelve years, you would get spousal support for four years. Find out what your state provides so there are no surprises. If it makes sense to change the default of the law in your state, get an agreement explicitly stating that fact.

Property Designation

One of the primary functions of a pre- or postnuptial agreement is to define what constitutes marital property and what is considered separate property. Marital property is what is divided between the parties in a property settlement at divorce. Separate property is, as it sounds, solely the owner's and not subject to distribution. A good example might be money you inherited from your grandparents. They clearly wanted their money to go to you. This is where the financial disclosure comes into play, because typically everything on that list is off-limits to the marital estate. Often an agreement will state that any increase in value of those separate premarital assets is off the table as well. If you think it best to underestimate values and not fully itemize assets, you will be sorry later because you will want to be sure more rather than less is defined as separate property.

Transmutation

Transmutation is when an asset is converted either from nonmarital to community property or vice versa. Transmutation usually must occur by title—a written document affirming the mutual agreement to the change in the property's character—or by commingling. If you live in one of the nine community property states (see the "Bankruptcy" section in Chapter 4 for a list) and you agree to maintain separate property, make sure your lawyer includes the clear provision that separate property does not transmute or transform into community property upon marriage or upon the non-owner spouse spending marital funds on that separate asset. A prenuptial agreement may specifically provide that property will not be considered community or marital property in the marital estate regardless of the contributions made by either party.

Debts

Often a pre- or postnuptial agreement specifies that any debts incurred by one party before or during the marriage do not become the obligations of the other party. That can be a very important provision in an agreement that could later be used to defend against the claims of a creditor going after assets of one spouse for the debt of the other. This is one of the reasons that the financial disclosure entered into as part of preparing the agreement must include not only an accurate list of all assets but also a full list of debts.

Right of First Refusal in the Home

The agreement can include a right of first refusal in the home, so it is clear who would have the initial option to keep the residence in the event of a split. There are basically three options for what can happen to the marital home at a split: he buys you out, you buy him out, or you sell the property and divide the proceeds. To the extent that this can be agreed upon at the outset, that explicit understanding most likely will save time and money should the relationship come to an end.

Handling Income

You will want to discuss how income earned during the marriage is handled. There are essentially two kinds of income: active (earned through employment or other intentional efforts) or passive (such as appreciation of real estate or investment accounts that increase in value over time and without specific effort). Will these forms of income be handled the same, and if so, will they be marital assets or remain separate? For example, even if you deposit your paycheck in a separate account in your name alone, absent an agreement otherwise, the law assumes that the income is still a marital asset and would have to be part of a property settlement on divorce.

Business Interests

Without a nuptial agreement, your spouse can obtain an interest in a business that you own or have an interest in. It is anathema to most families to think about co-owning a business with a former in-law; any such shares or partnership interest in a family business must be disclosed and specifically taken out of the picture for any property settlement. That goes for any enterprise you have any stake in. The business itself might be premarital, but most states say that the increase in value during the marriage is a marital asset. You might not want that asset on the table and subject to the total division of assets in the event of a divorce. In that case you would be entering the complex and expensive world of getting someone to assign a value to the business, and then having to buy out your spouse's interest through other marital assets or installment payments.

Commingling

Commingling means that you mix your nonmarital money in an account with marital money (and yes, your income is marital money once you get married if you do not have a prenup that provides otherwise), such that it is not clear which portion is marital and which is nonmarital. Think of two glasses of water being poured together into one glass—you cannot discern which water came from where. In a dissolution action, the account would be considered commingled and therefore marital, and then subject to litigation over whether it should be divided equally or not. If you get a creative lawyer and even a forensic accountant (rather like a detective specializing in investigating and tracking financial transactions), she might be able to make a successful claim for an offset of the dollars that you contributed. If you have that concern, it would be safer and less expensive to maintain in a separate account any funds you would want to walk out the door with. If you do not want to go through all of that, avoid commingling.

Inheritances and Gifts

Another provision that frequently appears in a nuptial agreement is that any inheritance or gift received by one party during the marriage does not become a marital asset. In many states, this is the default of the law, in the absence of an agreement about commingling, but it is a good idea to be clear if you are trying to keep any gifts or bequests separate.

Waiver of Automatic Retirement Benefits

If you want to give some or all of your retirement benefits to a person or entity that is not your spouse, that should be specified in a nuptial agreement. Remember my misinformed client Troy from the introduction? Had he put together a basic prenup before his marriage, he would have retained his complete interest in the retirement accounts he worked hard to build up.

Jackie and Lisa's Story

....

Jackie and Lisa did not enter into a prenup. When Jackie passed away, Lisa inherited Jackie's retirement accounts because Jackie had not had Lisa sign either a prenuptial agreement or a separate document waiving her interest in Jackie's retirement accounts. A prenuptial agreement could have memorialized the intention that Lisa not inherit from Jackie. When Jackie passed away, Lisa was able to inherit more than Jackie wanted and expected her to get, minimizing the share her daughters received.

Property Titling

Be sure to include what happens if you put your spouse on the title to the home that you owned before the marriage. You may not get back your share of the equity you had prior to that change, absent an agreement clearly stating that understanding. Without an agreement, it is a gift that transforms the assets into marital assets, and she could claim she has an equal interest in the home or is exclusively entitled to use and possession of the home during and after the divorce for a certain period of time.

Alternative Dispute Resolution

Do not forget to put a provision for alternative dispute resolution or other joint professionals (such as one neutral forensic accountant, one property appraiser) in the agreement. Rather than risking a conflict ending up in court, where the emotional and financial costs skyrocket, consider provisions for an escalating process of conflict resolution. A couples counselor should be sought to work things through at the outset. If that fails, a neutral mediator can attempt to help you come to a solution together. See if you can agree to a collaborative divorce process (check out the section "Collaborative Law" in Chapter 12). If none of these resolves the conflict, the next level could be an arbitrator, depending on your state's laws, who might be a retired judge or a qualified lawyer who issues a binding decision.

Understanding

Include language that each person is signing the agreement with a full understanding of its consequences, has had plenty of time to consider each provision before signing the agreement, and is comfortable with its contents. If English is not one spouse's first language, consider including a provision that the agreement was in some way translated so that there is no comprehension issue caused by a language barrier.

These agreements are important to get right, and there are many state-specific requirements. Do not risk the temptation to save money by using a boilerplate agreement. Finally, this book is not a substitute for legal advice. Do not think that between what you have learned here and what you find on the Internet, you will be able to create an agreement tailored to your specific circumstances and compliant with your state law. If you need a prenup or postnup, it is worth the professional attorney fees to get it right.

11
ORGANIZING YOUR FINANCES

There can be no disparity in marriage like unsuitability of
mind and purpose.

—*Charles Dickens*, David Copperfield

Many couples struggle with whether and how to merge finances.
You may be more comfortable commingling your finances and
sharing expenses. The ideal way to handle day-to-day living expenses is different for each couple. One option that seems to work
and reduces the nickel-and-diming of every date night, especially
where there is a disparity in earnings and assets, is to keep assets separate and then to open a joint house account and use the debit card
for meals together, groceries, and date nights. I call this the "hers,
mine, and ours" approach.

To manage this option, add up the shared expenses for a few
months, then create an average monthly expense budget. Each of
you contributes half of that amount to a joint account each month. If
there is a big difference in income, consider contributing a monthly
amount proportional to each person's earnings. This prorated
method is fair and appealing to many couples. Whether the relationship is new, you have very different spending habits, you have been
burned in the past, or you just prefer to "keep it clean," this practice
can be a relationship-saver.

Bruce and Miguel's Story

. . . .

Bruce's income is $130,000 annually; Miguel currently earns around $28,000. Bruce and Miguel have agreed that, even though Bruce owns the house, Miguel wants to contribute his share to the monthly upkeep. He does not want to feel as though he is being "kept." In devising their list of monthly household expenses, shown below, they agree to include the mortgage because Miguel would be paying rent regardless. However, they exempt homeowner's insurance, property taxes, water, sewer, garbage, and the costs of other big household improvements, which remain Bruce's individual expenses.

Also considered individual expenses are their car and car insurance payments, gasoline, personal care including medications, trips to the salon, clothing, health insurance premiums, gym membership, cell phone, and charitable donations. After reviewing all of their expenses, they conclude that their total average joint expenses are $7,000. Here is how it breaks down monthly:

Mortgage	$3,250
Gas and electricity	$170
Alarm system	$15
Internet and cable	$200
Landscaping	$300
House cleaning	$200
Groceries	$800
Pet care	$200
Dining out	$700
Entertainment (movies/theater, museums)	$65
Vacation	$600
Other	$500
Total	**$7,000**

With practice, the record-keeping and prorated spending becomes easier. It might take a few months to get into the swing of it and couples need not be miserly about making sure everything is perfectly equitable. After all, this is love! Love might also mean that things do not need to be precisely divided. Couples find the longer they are together the more they develop a shared understanding of how to spend money. Flexibility and shared financial priorities are the goal of the "hers, mine, and ours" approach.

HERS, MINE, AND OURS IN ACTION

Bruce and Miguel reviewed their ongoing expenses, determined which would be considered joint, crafted a monthly budget, and then divided into shares as follows:

	Bruce	Miguel	TOTAL
Net monthly income (take home pay)	$8,000	$2,000	$10,000
Joint **monthly house expenses**			$7,000
Percentage of financial responsibility (Divide Bruce's net monthly income by the total net monthly income to get Bruce's percentage of monthly expenses; divide Miguel's net monthly income by the total net monthly income to get Miguel's percentage of monthly expenses.)	80%	20%	100%
Share of monthly obligation (Multiply Bruce's percentage of financial responsibility by the monthly household expenses to get Bruce's share; multiply Miguel's percentage of financial responsibility by the monthly household expenses to get Miguel's share.)	$5,600	$1,400	$7,000
Remainder for personal expenses	$2,400	$600	

There's No Fair There

DAVID BOYER

Freelance radio producer

San Francisco, California, and Brooklyn, New York

For me, one of the best parts about being gay is the need to chart my own path without the prescribed guideposts that most heterosexuals must at the very least consider and then reject, accept, or amend. Kids, marriage, monogamy—for me, it's all up for grabs. In most cases, that is exactly how I like it. And for much of my adulthood, this free-form approach to life and love also suited my approach to my finances.

I grew up in a family where money seemed to guide most decisions and where outcomes were measured in dollars, so as an adult I took a somewhat different approach to financial matters. If there was money in the account when I keyed in my ATM code, then all was well. My retirement plan? A modest inheritance (hopefully), avoiding debt, and, well, never really retiring. This method worked well enough when I was single, but once I got into my first real relationship about ten years ago, this approach was incompatible with reality and my desire to connect in a deeper way.

The first signs of complexity came with the decision to move in together. When my now-ex and I met, we lived a block apart in apartments we each owned. Mine, per my MO, was small, sparse, and paid off. His was larger, nicer, and came with a sizable mortgage. What to do? Well, first things first: him moving into my place was a nonstarter. So either we had to continue to live nearby and apart or I was going to move in with him. If I moved in with him, I could rent my place out and pocket about a grand a month. But what would I contribute to his expenses? If I was helping him pay off his mortgage—and if he was getting a sizable tax deduction on the interest—what would "fair" look like?

Ah, that word, "fair." It's the gold standard of financial commingling, and yet it's incredibly subjective. I had seen it backfire on gay couples before. When my brother and his boyfriend of more than a decade split, there was no road map to fair. And what was "fair" when they were happy together was very different from the version of "fair" that emerged after an infidelity. At the time, watching him navigate that uncoupling made me envious of heterosexual, government-approved marriages (or at least divorces). The guidelines were so clear: 50/50 and no-fault, or whatever the prevailing state rules were. Instead, his boyfriend preemptively emptied their joint bank account for fear that my brother's version of fair and his had diverged.

In my own relationship, I sought second and third opinions as we decided that I would move into my then-boyfriend's place. It was not exactly romantic, but it was very conscious. We settled on a figure that was just a little less than half of his mortgage, and we opened a joint account into which we both deposited an equal amount each month. Once the decision was made, we never really talked about it again. When we split, there was little friction around finances. We did have to negotiate the divvying up of our art and housewares, but, I'm still proud to say, we did it with little arguing. I think it helped that our possessions did not become proxies within a larger, more complex negotiation of finances and "fairness."

Both my brother and I entered new relationships after those initial splits. My brother took the same approach as he had a decade earlier: he and his new partner planned to be "fair" if they were ever to split. Guess what: when they did eventually split after a decade, it was once again ugly. The definition of "fair" had shifted. Threats of legal action ensued. Once again I briefly considered the benefits of legally getting hitched.

As for my relationship, after two years we are just beginning to talk about moving in together. I am once again contemplating the benefits of a joint account. And as we begin to think about renting or buying, no doubt I will seek second and third opinions. What has changed since the last time I found myself at this crossroad? Marriage—legal and equal—is now possible. But my desire to eschew the guideposts and to avoid the conventional remains. What happens next? TBD. But one thing is certain: I will not rely on a vague, mushy concept of "fair." I will talk openly and specifically with my partner. And this time, who knows: there may even be a legally binding contract in place, be it a state-issued marriage license or something else altogether.

The Only Thing I Can Control Is the Laundry

HELEN SMOLINSKI

Mom and lawyer

Former Managing Director, Lawyers' Committee for Civil Rights of the San Francisco Bay Area

San Francisco, California

One of the jokes I tell as a fledgling stand-up comic, who has performed exactly *four* times in public, goes like this: My wife travels a lot for business. When she called home last night to say goodnight to the kids and me, she said it sounded like a 911 call: lots of screaming and crying in the background and me answering her questions about our day like she's an EMS dispatcher—one-word answers in between either consoling or yelling at the kids. Mostly yelling.

Suffice it to say that we have no idea what we're doing as parents. Our kids—twins, a boy and a girl—are five years old. You'd think we would have figured out some things by now, but that's the "fun" of parenting: once you've solved one problem, a new one arises. *It never stops.* Add to the mix the fact that our daughter is disabled, and we often feel like we are just hanging on.

When we were first reeling from the news about our daughter, friends and family encouraged us to attend a support group with other parents of disabled kids. We were reluctant to, mostly be-cause we were tired. But our friends persisted and our families insisted; all we heard from our loved ones was a chorus of "Go and you'll see you aren't alone!" So we went . . . *and we were the only ones who showed up to the meeting.* We really were alone!

It turns out our mistake was choosing a support group meet-ing in the middle of summer, a time when many families are away on vacation. We tried a few meetings later and found great solace in seeing other families like ours figure it out. The thing is, though, we were the only gay couple. I thought that would matter for some reason, but it didn't. It doesn't.

Truth be told, my wife and I are bad gays. We wanted to get married and have children since practically the day we met. There was never any hand-wringing for us about whether mar-riage would threaten our lesbian identities or corrupt our feminist values. We wanted marriage because it signaled commitment to us, and because that's what people did when they fell in love and wanted to spend the rest of their lives together. We identified with everyone else; why shouldn't we want marriage, too?

Of course, it helped tremendously that we met in 2004 and were living in San Francisco, arguably the exact time and place that the modern gay marriage movement was born. We had the privilege to believe it really was just a matter of time before marriage would be legal. We never thought for a second that we wouldn't be married one day—really, truly married. How's that for a sense of entitlement? Although, being more practical than romantic, I didn't want to get married in California if the federal government wasn't going to recognize our marriage, too. I knew filing tax returns was complicated enough without that added hurdle.

So we waited. Instead, we became "domestic partners" in Cali-fornia (a term that, thankfully, already sounds dated) so that my now-wife could more easily adopt our children. Our twins were born in 2010; we had to wait until 2013 before we could get mar-ried in California *and* have the federal government recognize our marriage as legal, too. We wanted all this now to protect our kids.

It should come as no surprise, then, that after I gave birth to our twins, we found ourselves following another traditional path: I stayed home to be the primary caregiver, while my wife continued to work full-time and support us all. It wasn't our initial plan, however.

I remember my mom asking us while I was pregnant why we were having kids if we weren't planning on one of us staying home with them. My wife and I thought at the time: "Oh, how old-fashioned of her! Of course we are going back to work after maternity leave, because we are modern career women and this is what we do."

But then we learned I was carrying twins. And suddenly it made more sense financially for me to leave my job as a public interest lawyer and stay home to care for two infants than to put them in day care. Besides, I didn't want them in day care. I wanted to stay home with our babies, and my wife wanted to keep working at her job. Most crucially, we were lucky enough to have a rent-controlled apartment (a one-bedroom, but still), which made it all possible.

I planned on only staying home for a year at most. But then we discovered our daughter suffers from a physically and mentally debilitating genetic disorder that makes her dependent on others for all activities of daily living. I'm now on year five. I stay home to care for our daughter. I also stay home to care for our son, who's healthy. And I love it! As hard as it is, I am grateful that I didn't miss out on this opportunity to be home with my kids. My wife continues to work full-time and loves what she does. Our arrangement works for our family because my wife and I each believe the other has the harder job!

We didn't set out with this arrangement in mind; we fell into it out of necessity, circumstance, and a little preference, the way I imagine it works for most families when figuring out how to live day-to-day. We didn't have to reinvent the wheel. The so-called traditional familial arrangement we've adopted is really just about a division of labor. That being said, I think my wife does more around the house than she might if she were a man precisely because she is a woman and was raised as a woman. She is well versed in the amount of work it takes to raise children and keep house; this is why she doesn't see me as "not working." She knows I work very hard taking care of our family and that's why neither of us has to ask before spending money from our joint bank account. We each appreciate what the other contributes to our family. Of course, it also helps that we share the same financial values, too.

Is it all still incredibly difficult? Of course, but parenting is difficult, life is difficult. I honestly don't know how any of us does it. Gay parents, straight parents, single parents, with or without special-needs kids—aren't we all just hanging on? But we persist. We persist because the good outweighs the bad on some days (if we're lucky, most days) and because our kids need us. As hard as it is, it is my great privilege and honor to be my kids' primary caregiver. Now, excuse me—I have to get the laundry out of the dryer.

12
DIVORCE

The biggest financial pitfall in life is divorce. And the biggest reason for divorce is marriage.

—Gene Simmons

*B*efore I Do is a guide to the legal aspects of marriage; it is not a guide to divorce. But one cannot talk about one and not the other. One of the major legal benefits of marriage is divorce. Now LGBT people are able to not only get *into* but also get *out of* our marriages.

Studies show that same-sex couples' marriages dissolve at a slightly lower rate than heterosexual couples'. This may be in part due to the fact that by the time many of us were legally able to marry, we already had been together for many years, if not decades. Many couples have survived several seven-year itches before legal marriage was possible. Social scientists estimate that this disparity will disappear in the future and that divorce rates will equalize.

Before we enjoyed nationwide marriage equality, some married same-sex couples found themselves "wedlocked"—living in a state sans marriage equality that therefore would not dissolve same-sex marriages legally entered into in another state. With marriage equality the law of the land, we now can divorce where we live.

IF YOU ARE CONTEMPLATING DIVORCE:
THREE ACTIONS

If your marriage is coming to an end, there are three things you will want to do lickety-split. First, as soon as possible, sit down with a family lawyer who has worked with same-sex couples. There are essentially two ways to divorce: amicably or adversarially. If you are getting along, have no assets or debts together, and have no children, you might be able to do a simple uncontested divorce; these types of divorce are very affordable. If you have kids, lots to divide, and/or you and your spouse are not on the same page, those factors could lead to a dissolution that is more of an emotional and financial investment. Either way, it can be fruitful to have an immediate consultation, even if just for one or two hours, with a family lawyer who will flag any potential issues and help you come up with a basic road map to divorce.

Second, if there is a reasonable fear of bad financial behavior from your soon-to-be ex, you may want to close any joint credit card accounts. A jilted partner with your credit card can do damage—and you are legally responsible for those debts. A "shopportunity" at your expense is only going to exacerbate the acrimony. If you are nervous that your spouse might clean out bank accounts and move the money out of the country or leave automatic deductions piling up to an overdrawn account, beat your spouse to it and empty them yourself. In order to not face any allegations of stealing money that legally belongs to both of you, consider placing those funds in your lawyer's trust account or in some other safe escrow situation with a neutral party, such as the real estate lawyer who handled the closing for your home. You could ask the bank to put a freeze on the account, but some of my clients have found that then unfreezing it is more difficult than expected. The safe placement of any contestable joint funds can give you peace of mind while the divorce proceeds. Secure any and all valuable possessions that you would miss if your ex had a destructive temper tantrum. If your grandmother's china is dear to you, or if you do not have scanned versions of prior tax returns or other important records, get those off the shared premises and into a safe place. A short-term storage unit to which only you have access can be a great option. It is easier to resolve the conflicts without added fallout from the impetuous acts of an aggrieved spouse.

Third, examine your estate planning documents. Even while you are separated and moving toward dissolution of the marriage, these documents are effective unless specifically revoked or amended.

Quickly revoke your durable power of attorney. Inform any banks or other entities that have been given a copy; if they have been notified of the revocation, they are liable for any losses if they subsequently rely on that document. If you do not revoke your durable power of attorney, your ex could march into a bank and clean out your account. That action would be a breach of fiduciary duty, and you would probably win a suit for the return of those funds, but it would be an aggravating and costly battle. At the same time, change your advance directives so that your ex does not have the power to make medical decisions for you. Designate someone else immediately.

Promptly redo your testamentary documents as well so that your spouse is no longer your personal representative, trustee, or beneficiary. In most states, if you die and never make these changes, the law presumes that you would not want your ex-spouse to inherit from you or serve as a fiduciary. In the case of divorce, if your ex should die with those old documents in place, the proceeds of her estate would go to the next person in line after you. However, that only happens when the divorce is final. If the process is a protracted one and you should pass away while the case is still pending, your ex could still be appointed to administer your estate and receive the bequests planned while all was rosy.

HOW IT WORKS, AND WHAT'S STILL DIFFERENT FOR US

Each of the fifty states and the District of Columbia has different laws about marriage and divorce. The widespread availability of divorce for same-sex couples does not mean we have smooth sailing ahead. It is great to no longer be "wedlocked," but the years during which we could not marry might still impact that divorce. Divorce is difficult no matter how you slice it. Having complex issues mucking things up does not help.

This section provides a broad overview of these laws. In some states, alimony is awarded for long-term and not for short-term marriages; what constitutes "long-term" varies. Alimony is generally awarded when one spouse is in need of support and the other spouse has the ability to pay that support.

In the absence of a nuptial agreement, the assets and debts of a marriage are divided equitably, and usually equally, though many states allow for a spouse to argue he is entitled to more than half. This split is more or less how it boils down both in the nine states that have community property and the remaining forty-one states and the District of Columbia, which have equitable distribution. The basic difference between those two is that with equitable distribution, there is a more of an inquiry into what each person earned and contributed to the marital assets and brought to the marriage, as well as the duration of the marriage. In community property states, the presumption is that everything is equal and it does not matter who contributed what. There are, however, cases in community property states where one party can, with meticulous record keeping, track the source of the contested property to a separate asset and therefore take property off the marital table.

A complicated issue that sometimes arises when a couple has been together for many years before marrying is what is known as the "date of marriage." The date of marriage is, as it sounds, the date that a couple entered into legal matrimony. It impacts which assets are deemed to be "of the marriage" and which ones are premarital and therefore not subject to division in a divorce (except for when they are). These issues are often thorny and not clear-cut. Is the date of marriage considered the date of the marriage license from the other state, or the date when the marriage was recognized by the couple's state of residence, if those are not one and the same? We urge lawyers and clients to use the date of the marriage license, so that people are not trying to use the history of homophobic laws to their strategic advantage.

Another complication arises when a couple has been together for many years but only married for a short time. The disparity between the length of legal marriage and the longer relationship can impact both the division of marital property and the determination of spousal support obligation. Let's say you and your honey have been together for twenty years. Ten years ago you agreed that you would quit working to focus on running the home or raising the children. Last year you were finally able to marry. If you split up tomorrow, you would be deemed to have been married for only a year. Most judges decide on spousal support based on the length of the marriage. In this case, spousal support would be unlikely after only one year of marriage. Judges usually have discretion to look at the big picture, however, and do what is fair. A savvy lawyer might successfully argue that your relationship was indeed long-term and that the arrangement to sacrifice your career was a mutual one made a decade prior, when you did not yet have the option to enter into a legal marriage.

Same-sex couples who have been together for many years and live in one of the places that recognize common-law marriage (Alabama, Colorado, District of Columbia, Iowa, Kansas, Montana, Oklahoma, Rhode Island, South Carolina, Texas, and Utah) have another potential argument to bolster their divorce case. These states regard relationships that look like a marriage as tantamount to a marriage. There are a few other states which recognize common-law marriages if commenced before a certain date: that date is in the 1990s for Georgia, Idaho, and Ohio, and 2003 for Pennsylvania. Some states will recognize a common-law marriage if the couple moved from a state that recognized their common-law marriage. If you are going through a divorce and your situation would benefit from a longer-term marriage than that of your legal union, consider whether you live or lived in a place with common-law marriage recognition. If so, and if you have been together long enough to qualify, seek out the services of a sharp attorney who can help craft an argument that you presented yourselves as a married couple and evidenced intent to be married for much longer than the legal marriage.

The date of marriage is important because it characterizes what property is part of the overall marital estate and can establish entitlement or a defense to a claim of alimony. While the law varies from state to state, marital assets are typically divided equally upon divorce. What constitutes a marital asset is based on the date of marriage.

Tania and Marie's Story

• • • • • • • • • • • •

Tania and Marie had been together since 1997 and married since 2005. While they were together, they figured it made most sense to use Marie's income to pay the household bills and use as much of Tania's income as possible to max out Tania's retirement account. Tania had taken over the family business and instituted a generous retirement savings program with employer matching benefits. When they got together and promised eternal love and partnership back in 1997, Tania's retirement account had a balance of $5,000. When they married in 2005, Tania's account was up to $100,000. At the time of the divorce in 2013, the balance was $220,000. Where Marie and Tania live, Marie is entitled to half of the increase in value. Given the date of marriage, the increase in value is $120,000, the amount that accrued over the term of the eight-year marriage. If they had married back in 1997, Marie would be entitled to half of the $215,000 increase in value. If the divorce judge considers the date of marriage to be 2005, Marie will walk away with just $60,000 from that account. If she considers 1997 the date of marriage, Marie will receive $107,500.

Bruce and Miguel's Story

• • • • • • • • • • • • •

Bruce and Miguel were residents of Virginia who married at their second home in Delaware in August 2013. The marriage was rushed and they were very sure they would be together forever, so they did not think about a prenuptial agreement to memorialize their intentions should the relationship end. Bruce owns properties, and he has bank and retirement accounts, all of which he acquired before his marriage to Miguel. Bruce sold the Rehoboth Beach cottage in the winter of 2014 and put the cash in their joint account. As the relationship unraveled through the summer of 2014 and before he filed for divorce that December, Bruce moved the proceeds of the real estate sale from the joint account to an account in his name alone and claimed those dollars were nonmarital assets.

Marriage equality became the law of Virginia in October 2014. Bruce and Miguel's marriage, however, was legally solemnized in Delaware fourteen months prior, a month after it became legal in Delaware. Bruce argues that his actions all took place before their marriage was legally recognized in their home state of Virginia and therefore are of no significance in a divorce case. That is an awfully homophobic position to take. They entered into their marriage knowing it was legal. If he wanted to be sure that there was *no presumption that those funds were marital, he should have initiated an agreement to that effect and should not have commingled those funds. A judge should rule those funds as a marital asset.*

Commingling, the mixing of marital and nonmarital funds in an account, is important. In general, funds that might have not been joint assets become assets of the marriage when they are placed in a joint account or when marital monies, such as income earned during the marriage, are deposited into an account with nonmarital funds. If one spouse sells a house that he owned before the marriage and puts the proceeds in a joint account held with the other spouse, the character of those funds changes in that instant from nonmarital to marital. In the divorce, the spouse who did not own the house could make a claim that he is entitled to half of the proceeds.

People splitting up often seem to be of the impression that they cannot move out of a shared home. They think that if they do they will be forfeiting their rights in the jointly owned home. Stop getting your legal advice from the TV or Internet! Generally, moving out of a home does not constitute abandonment. For the most part, if you choose to move out, you are not giving up any rights to the marital home. If you voluntarily leave the residence, you could be held liable for its continued upkeep, which you might be able to negotiate as an offset in the context of the overall property settlement—meaning that you might not need to pay those upkeep expenses out of pocket but rather can pay less as part of the overall deal. Your responsibility is usually limited to the mortgage, homeowner's insurance, and major maintenance. You do not necessarily need to pay for your ex's cable, electric, and water bills when you do not live there, though you should consult with an attorney to determine what a court would likely hold you responsible to pay during the proceedings and what is a fair temporary resolution.

However, if you are denied entry to a shared home, that is called "ouster," and you might argue that you cannot be expected to be responsible for the expenses of the home when you are forced to pay for your own housing. Proving ouster, however, can be difficult. Were the locks changed? Do you have a text or email that makes it crystal clear you are not welcome to come home? These actions can be considered proof.

Another way in which divorce is different for same-sex couples is the need to be mindful of the various forms of relationship recognition that have been available to us over time. If you are divorcing, be sure to dissolve each legal status, not just the marriage. Do not think that just because you are now in a legally recognized marriage, that trumps whatever other statuses you might have entered into elsewhere. Nor does a divorce magically terminate those other forms of relationship recognition unless the divorce decree is properly worded. Each status needs to be visited individually.

Determining Status

DEBORAH WALD

Chair, National Family Law Advisory Council for the National Center for Lesbian Rights

Wald Law Group

San Francisco, California

An often overlooked area of complexity facing family law attorneys in same-sex dissolutions involves accurately identifying the marital, domestic partnership, and/or civil union status of one's client. A family law attorney may go through his entire career without ever encountering a heterosexual client who legitimately does not know whether or not she is married. For lesbian and gay couples, this is not true. Given the myriad different statuses available to lesbian and gay couples over the past decade, and the speed with which these statuses and their legal meanings have changed, many clients will be completely unable to provide accurate information to their attorneys regarding their legal statuses. It is the job of the attorney to ask enough of the right questions to help the clients figure this out.

For example, based on options available in different states and countries over the past decade, a lesbian or gay man could be in any of at least six different statuses: (1) not in a legal union of any kind; (2) in a domestic partnership or civil union status created by their employer, municipality, or state that is *not* equivalent to a marriage; (3) in a state-registered domestic partnership that is equivalent to a marriage; (4) in a state-registered civil union that is equivalent to a marriage; (5) in a foreign relationship that may or may not be equivalent to a marriage (e.g., a German "registered life partnership"); or (6) married.

It is important to note here that none of the above statuses (except "not in a legal union of any kind") is mutually exclusive of the others. A California same-sex couple may well have registered as domestic partners in California, entered into a civil union in Vermont, *and* married in Canada. And, just to make sure they were truly married, they may have married *again* under California law once full marriage equality came to California. This raises several thought-provoking legal issues for an attorney handling a dissolution.

Chad and DeAndre are a gay couple who have been together for thirty-three years and reside in San Francisco. They held a wedding in 1990, on their ten-year anniversary, to which they invited their friends and family. Rings were exchanged at this time. When Vermont started allowing same-sex couples to enter into civil unions in 2000, they flew to Vermont to admire the foliage and enter into a civil union. When Massachusetts legalized marriage for same-sex couples in 2004, they got married during a festive weekend in Provincetown. When California made state-registered domestic partnerships equivalent to marriages in 2005, they registered with the secretary of state's office as domestic partners. When the California Supreme Court ruled that same-sex couples had a constitutional right to marry in 2008, they married again in the splendor of San Francisco City Hall.

Now, sadly, they are breaking up. What is their legal status? What is their date of marriage? How many separate relationships must be pled in their petition for dissolution? A family law attorney will have a choice of at least five different dates for the "date of marriage." Many California attorneys will want to use the 2004 Massachusetts marriage as the key date on a divorce petition, while others may not list a marriage date prior to the marriage first recognized by California in 2008. In reality, the appropriate "date of marriage" for Chad and DeAndre is the 2000 date upon which they entered into their Vermont civil union, since that is the date upon which they first entered into a relationship that is equivalent to marriage. The fact that the civil union was not recognized as a marriage equivalent in California until 2005 does not make a difference now that the Vermont civil union unquestionably will be recognized by a California court.

But Chad and DeAndre are unlikely to have a clue what date to use on their divorce petition, and if the divorce is not highly amicable, the one who would stand to benefit financially from a longer marriage may want to date the marriage all the way back to their wedding in 1990 (which may, in fact, be the most equitable answer, depending on the circumstances, and potentially would be legally correct in a state that recognizes common-law marriage), while the other likely will want to push the date out to 2008. Family law attorneys representing clients like Chad or DeAndre will need to fully understand the number and types of relationships their clients have entered into and help their clients determine what, in fact, is the operative "date of marriage" for dissolution purposes.

One other note about Chad and DeAndre: a dissolution of their marriage will effectively dissolve both the Massachusetts marriage and the California marriage, but it will not dissolve either their California domestic partnership or their Vermont civil union. Each of those relationships will need to be separately pled in court and separately adjudged dissolved in the judgment. Listing each separate marital-equivalent relationship with particularity in the pleadings and requesting dissolution of each and every one of these relationships is essential to actually ending the legal relationship between the parties and allowing each of them to once again hold the status of "single." A couple dissolving their marriage(s) but leaving their civil union and/or domestic partnership intact runs the risk that a subsequent marriage will be bigamous—and an attorney allowing that to happen runs the risk of committing malpractice.

ALIMONY

Alimony is also known as spousal maintenance or spousal support. It is typically taxable to the payee and deductible to the payor. The standard for how much is paid is based upon the payee's need and the payor's ability to pay. For the most part, there is no magic number of years of marriage after which alimony is automatically due upon divorce, although judges do consider the length of the marriage when faced with a request for spousal support. As previously discussed, this is a potentially complicated area for same-sex couples, many of whom have been together for many decades before marrying.

Are We Not the Marrying Kind?

FREDERICK HERTZ

Attorney and mediator

Author, *A Legal Guide for Lesbian & Gay Couples* and *Making It Legal: A Guide to Same-Sex Marriage, Domestic Partnerships & Civil Unions*

Oakland, California

A while back my partner asked me what it means to get married, legally speaking. I responded by explaining the rules this way: "If I support you for twenty years and you leave me, I'll have to support you for another ten." He replied (playfully, I'm sure), "Sounds great. Where do I sign up?"

Of all the indignities that lesbian and gay male divorced people complain about, paying spousal support (also known as alimony or maintenance) tops the charts. The litany of outrage follows some familiar patterns: "Why should I suffer for having supported him in the past? I did not suggest he quit his job." "She's the one who chose to leave me, so why should I be punished financially?" "He didn't give up anything to marry me—he was a loser financially well before we met!"

In many instances these spouses have good reason to complain. Their romantic relationship probably did not follow conventional heterosexual marriage patterns. Moreover, many likely got married as part of a civil rights celebration—not because they ever intended to sign up for these old-fashioned legal rules.

The historic rationale justifying the laws imposing alimony in straight divorces is twofold: first, there's a perception that the higher-income husband only was able to rise to the top with the love and support of his devoted homemaker wife, and second, the wife probably made career sacrifices to take care of the family, and so it would be unfair to toss her out empty-handed after years of devotion. Thus, the burden of alimony was part of the broader gender-based allocation of social roles.

Therein lies the problem. At least for now, most same-sex partnerships do not follow these sorts of traditional arrangements, simply because fewer same-sex couples raise children, and they certainly do not allocate responsibilities based upon gender. Instead, when there's economic inequality it typically arises from factors of health, class, ambition, choice of career, or simply good luck. Because the income differential was not the result of a conscious family arrangement, the legal burdens of alimony do not make much sense.

As I constantly remind my clients, there is no such thing as "gay marriage." Instead, we have opted into the existing heteronormative system of family law as it has developed over the centuries. Unfortunately for many of my clients (though it is welcome news for their financially dependent spouses), there is no "lesbian husband" exception to the spousal support rules. At least so far, I have never heard of a judge creating a gay exception to the standard legal divorce rules—and you should not expect that to happen, either.

If it is any comfort, I'm beginning to sense that, perhaps surprisingly, there may be some long-term benefits from the alimony rules for both partners. Facing the potential burden of paying spousal support might make the higher-income partner think differently when it comes to helping his or her spouse complete his education or pursue a career. It reinforces the notion that by getting married, you are now part of a family—a unified economic unit—with shared responsibilities and a shared future. In many ways, the law is pushing our families closer together, even when we did not think of our relationships in that way, and even if things go awry in the relationship.

And that may end up being a very good thing!

RETIREMENT ACCOUNTS

A bright spot in the divorce landscape for same-sex couples is the ability to divide retirement accounts in a tax-free way using a qualified domestic relations order (QDRO). A QDRO is a court order created in connection with a divorce. It allows the account holder to transfer a portion or all of the retirement account into the name of the other spouse without penalty or tax consequences if the transfer is being made as part of a divorce settlement. A QDRO is a highly technical document, prepared by a lawyer with specific experience and in consultation with the financial institution that holds the retirement account. It ensures that the withdrawal complies with the laws governing these accounts and the financial institution's specific requirements.

Retirement accounts have restrictions in terms of when we can access them and for what purposes. These restrictions protect us, preventing us from squandering our savings. For many couples, retirement accounts are their largest assets. When we could not avail ourselves of family law to dissolve our unions, the division of funds in a retirement account would come with stiff penalties and taxes for accessing these protected funds. A QDRO avoids those penalties.

TAX LIABILITY FROM MARRIAGE

In the course of or after splitting up (or perhaps as part of the very cause of that breakup), you might learn that your spouse has either lied or been mistaken in reporting something on your joint tax returns, resulting in a substantial tax bill in both names. If you had no idea about the error, you can seek what's known as "innocent spouse relief" from the IRS to shift the burden of this tax debt to your ex. Innocent spouse relief must be sought within two years of the IRS commencing efforts to collect against you. Innocent spouse relief is available only if you are divorced or legally separated, or if the spouse whose error triggered the joint liability has died.

COLLABORATIVE LAW

Collaborative law is an alternative dispute resolution technique sweeping the nation. If you are splitting up, consider it as a way to handle your divorce. The collaborative approach to problem solving is part of the discipline of therapeutic jurisprudence, which seeks to restore the law to the helping profession it once was before we became such a litigious society. Not only does it reduce the emotional and financial costs of divorce, but it also greatly increases the likelihood that you will not spend eternity wishing a violent death to befall your ex. Collaborative law is not ideal for every couple, particularly when there is a history of abuse or other problematic power dynamics, such as one spouse who holds all the assets and has a nasty habit of dishonesty. For many divorcing couples, however, collaborative law is a great alternative. Collaborative law requires a mental shift. With this approach, marriage is not a pie to be divided, so that the larger your ex's piece is, the smaller yours is. Rather, a collaborative divorce requires both parties to take a long-term view of the relationship and create a path to resolution that harms no one.

Collaborative Law

MARIETTE GELDENHUYS

Attorney and mediator

Founder, Ithaca Area Collaborative Law Professionals

Ithaca, New York

One of the most important choices a divorcing couple makes is the legal process they use. Many couples do not even realize that they have a choice; they each go to a divorce lawyer, who files for divorce in court or tries to settle the case by communicating with the other lawyer, with the threat of going to court if settlement demands are not met. This adversarial contest is ill-suited to the varied and complex legal, financial, and emotional issues divorcing families face. The concepts of "winning" and "losing" are meaningless when applied to family relationships. The legal process can cause irreparable damage to both spouses and their children. This is particularly true of same-sex couples, who still have unique legal issues that the legal system cannot adequately address, even after the advent of same-sex marriage.

Fortunately, collaborative law gives divorcing couples a way to work out the issues resulting from their divorce in a respectful and creative way, without going to court, and with the support of professionals who are trained to help them not only solve their immediate issues but also plan for the future. This process gives their family the best chance of successfully transitioning from one to two households.

The core of a collaborative law process is that the clients and their attorneys all commit to working out a settlement in joint meetings without going to court. The meetings are focused on the short- and long-term goals, needs, and interests of each spouse and their children. Attorneys receive special training so that they can guide their clients toward settlement in a less adversarial way than the traditional divorce model. The attorneys are focused solely on settlement and cannot go to court or threaten to do so. In the rare instances where a settlement is not reached and a client decides to go to court, both spouses must hire different lawyers. This ensures that the process is confidential and that clients do not have to worry that what they say in the meetings could possibly be used in court at a later time. Mental health professionals can help parents reach a parenting agreement and work out co-parenting issues, and they can act as coaches to help both spouses process the emotional aspects of their divorce so that they can have productive negotiations. Financial professionals can help gather and compile financial information, prepare budgets, and make financial projections to make sure that the settlement will work into the future. The way a professional team is assembled varies in each community of collaborative professionals.

The legal rules are part of the spouses' discussion, but unlike with a judge in a court case, the couple can decide to come up with their own solutions that meet their needs and interests. This is crucial to same-sex couples, where the legal system is often a poor fit for their situation.

The rules about division of property and debts are often based on the date when a couple got married. That works well for people who marry in the early stages of their relationship, before they accumulated much property and before they had children. However, until recently, same-sex couples were unable to marry. This means that they often get married many years into their relationship. If only the years of marriage count when deciding how to divide their property and whether one spouse needs support from the other, it can benefit one spouse and unfairly disadvantage the other spouse. In collaborative law, spouses can choose to honor the full duration of their relationship, rather than applying legal rules that lead to unfair results.

Existing legal rules also often do not treat both parents in a same-sex couple fairly. If there is only one legal parent and that parent chooses to take advantage of the legal system's unfair rules, it could have devastating consequences for the children and the other parent. In a collaborative law process, with the help of mental health professionals, parents are guided to understand the importance of their children's attachment to both parents and can work out a parenting plan that meets their children's needs. Collaborative law attorneys with expertise in LGBT family law can also help the parents figure out the best way for both parents to become legally recognized parents.

While there are no guarantees, couples who choose the collaborative process have the opportunity to preserve a civil relationship with each other and a healthy co-parenting relationship if they have children. They can plan for the future and come up with an agreement that will last, because they carefully weighed different options and made decisions based on solid information about their present and future needs.

Collaborative law, as you can imagine, is a fantastic tool to keep costs and emotions down. It is very versatile and gaining popularity.

13
ASSEMBLING A TEAM

Alone we can do so little. Together we can do so much.

—*Helen Keller*

It takes a village to handle much of what this book discusses. Do not be intimidated. Do not think you need to begin immediately to put together an arsenal of professionals to serve your every possible need. The key is finding the right people for the right purpose at the right time. Remember, professionals all have different areas of focus and expertise. Some tax professionals specialize in individual tax returns; others work primarily with corporate entities. Therapists might prefer to work with individuals, couples, or groups, with youths or adults. It is usually best when professionals "stay in their lane," that is, stick to what they do best. Resist the temptation to get comfortable with one person and lean on her to handle matters beyond her expertise.

Certainly lawyers have specific practice areas. Use caution if a lawyer professes to be proficient in everything you need. Those are referred to as "door" lawyers, because they will take whatever walks in the door. Just as you would not want to trust a neurologist to do your prostate exam, do not let your real estate lawyer handle an immigration case, unless it is crystal clear that immigration is also an area of major focus in her law practice. Why risk spending your hard-earned money to create more problems and not fix the pending one?

The importance of having quality professionals in your corner cannot be overstated. On these matters of grave personal significance, it is essential to work with someone who has not just a passing familiarity with your issue but understands the nuances as well. A professional need not be gay to serve you effectively, but you certainly deserve to feel understood when going through major life moments. You want someone who is well informed and up to date about the myriad issues affecting LGBT people and our families. Just because someone is gay himself does not mean he is well suited to assist you in your specific matter.

When seeking a professional to assist you, ask friends, colleagues, and even exes for referrals. Ask professionals you trust for referrals to those they trust. In addition to word of mouth, solicit information directly from the professional yourself. Have a consultation. Most professionals will charge for their time for a consultation since they are usually also providing services and dispensing advice during your meeting, but it is typically worth spending the few hundred dollars to see if it is a fit. It might even make sense to meet with two or three potential candidates, especially if your matter is complicated. These are deeply important and personal relationships—do not just go with the first name you get. You might want to just hire the most expensive person in town, figuring she is the best. Instead, think about choosing the professional who is the most responsive and with whom you connect.

Beware of what has become known in the LGBT community as the "bandwagon effect." This refers to those Johnny-come-latelies who realize that our community represents a potential income source and jump on the bandwagon to solicit our business. Choose professionals with the depth of experience and understanding that you deserve. These are critical and intimate issues; do not cut corners. If you think you don't want to spend the money to hire a seasoned professional, wait until you see how much it costs when you hire an amateur.

With regard to LGBT sensitivity, none of these are deal breakers, but these questions offer some guidance on how to gauge a professional's authenticity:

- How long has the professional been working with the LGBT community?
- What specific experience does he or she have in working with our families?
- Is there substantial content about LGBT involvement on the professional's website? Has the professional served on boards or committees, and generally given time, talent, and treasure to the community?
- Do marketing photos and visual images include at least one same-sex couple or family?
- Do intake forms refer inclusively to a variety of family formations?
- Does the professional write and speak publicly about LGBT issues with regularity?
- If there are LGBT-specific affiliations or certifications in the practice area, does she have them? For example, lawyers can be members of the National LGBT Bar Association, which has a Family Law Institute for which applicants must be vetted as having sufficient experience working with our families.

Financial advisors can get an Accredited Domestic Partner Advisor (ADPA) designation. While someone *not* having this designation does not necessarily mean there is a lack of familiarity with our community's issues, in a sea of financial advisors who are interested in marketing to the LGBT community, obtaining and maintaining the ADPA designation shows a commitment to becoming and staying informed. As we have shifted to nationwide marriage equality and domestic partnerships are phasing out as a relationship status, this designation has become less common and, many feel, less necessary. This is unfortunate. Our community's uniqueness can be subsumed by professionals suggesting that "it's all the same now." With nationwide marriage equality and the increasing mainstreaming of LGBT couples, it can be harder to identify those financial advisors and other professionals who have true capacity and sensitivity for same-sex couples and the unique legal needs we still face.

The Shifting Landscape of Financial Planning for LGBT Clients After Marriage Equality

NAN P. BAILEY MBA, CFP, AIF

Financial advisor

NPB Wealth Management

New York, New York

I have served as a financial advisor to many lesbian and gay couples over age fifty, most of whom had assumed that marriage equality would not come in our lifetime. This assumption has fostered a strong sense of independence, as much out of need as circumstance. What it also led to was a practice of defining our relationships as seemed fit. Over the years, clients have come in with a variety of different partnership agreements, formalized or not, reflected in their division of household expenses, responsibilities, and provisions in the event of death.

Most of my straight couples (and younger gay couples) tend to assume that all assets and earned income are shared by the household. Alternatively, older married lesbian and gay couples are sometimes hesitant or slow to commingle income and investments, even though they now enjoy unlimited gifting as a couple and must file joint tax returns. It is not unusual to prepare three sets of retirement projections for a same-sex couple: two plans for each as individuals and one combined plan. Marriage equality poses such a dramatic paradigm shift—it takes a lot to absorb and appreciate all the implications.

Uncovering financial planning opportunities that are unique to the LGBT community has been a theme in my practice. I have come across lesbian couples where one partner is a widow, having once been married to a husband who is now deceased. If she is not working or has less than $15,720 earned income (in 2016), she can claim Social Security survivor benefits on her deceased ex-husband's account as early as age sixty, as long as she has not remarried before age sixty. Accordingly, I have had same-sex clients postpone wedding plans till after age sixty!

In the spring of 2012, a client was referred to me after his spouse had died in February of that year. The survivor was required to roll over his spouse's employer's retirement benefits to an inherited IRA within sixty days of the date of death. Because the *Windsor* case was before the Supreme Court at the time, we were able to request the funds be rolled into a spousal inherited IRA. The IRA custodian agreed—though they did request a copy of the marriage certificate. Since the survivor was in his early fifties, this has prevented the survivor from many years of taking required minimum distributions that would have been taxable on top of his current earnings—a classic example of the discrimination felt by same-sex couples before the Supreme Court ruling allowed for marriage recognition on the federal level.

Some of the checklist items for LGBT couples considering marriage or newly married clients are:

- For two-income couples, marriage will usually increase their income taxes, but the unlimited marital deduction for estate/gift taxes can be a significant benefit.
- Once you are married, resubmit beneficiary designations to specify that your partner is now your spouse. Spousal beneficiary options can be much more favorable and less onerous in taxes.
- Consider changing real property from joint tenants with rights of survivorship to joint tenants by entirety (only available to married couples) for added asset protection.

It is a good idea to work with a tax professional who is familiar with some of the perks and pitfalls of being a same-sex couple, in order to evaluate your financial situation before marrying and to prepare your taxes annually. Yes, there are great online tax preparation tools that might be tempting to use if your income is modest, but the tax ramifications of marriage are serious, and the opportunities for creativity are numerous (see Karen Stogdill's excellent cameo, "I Do, Mr. Taxman: How Marital Status Can Impact Your Taxes" in Chapter 4). Errors are less likely when using a tax preparer. With professional assistance, you are also better able to navigate the dizzying system of bonuses, deductions, and credits available to married couples.

14
HAPPILY EVER AFTER

L GBT people fought for the right to marry for over four decades. I personally fought for marriage equality in the state of Florida. Yet in this book I slap a big yellow "handle with care" sticker all over marriage, the institution LGBT people struggled to enter. My most sincere apologies to readers who feel I have rained all over the marriage parade. This information is just too darn important to gloss over with a rainbow flag. Many of these lessons apply to all couples, gay or straight, who decide to get serious, move in together, and take their relationships to the next level with legal recognition. My colleagues and I have all seen far too many disastrous consequences from marriages that were rushed into—by straight and gay couples alike.

Congratulations on reading this book. It bodes well for your relationship that you have been willing to embrace reality over fantasy. It bodes well for the LGBT community as a whole that we are thinking about ways to understand the institution of marriage and make it work for our modern lives. We can still be romantic and have meaningful rituals while being thoughtful about the whole enterprise. Perhaps gay and lesbian people can rehabilitate the institution of marriage, as we have done to many neighborhoods we have moved into and made even more fabulous!

I hope this snapshot of the myriad issues that can arise around marriage has given you food for thought. Use all that you have learned here to be aware and make responsible choices. When you assemble your own team—lawyer, accountant, mental health professional, financial advisor—be prepared with questions and concerns pertinent to your state and your circumstances.

In summary, here are key points to remember before you say "I do":

- Marry after deliberation.
- Marry after talking to an accountant.
- Marry after talking with your partner about it a lot. *A lot.*
- Do not marry as a political statement.
- Do not marry because it is a fun excuse for a big party.
- Do not marry because you have kids and they deserve married parents. (That argument is infuriating. Where does that leave—among others—single moms, unmarried straight couples, or all the same-sex couples who have been parenting for decades without the right to marry and have done a perfectly excellent job at it?)
- Do not marry because everyone is asking you when you are going to marry and what could possibly be the reason for waiting other than you are on the fence about your relationship.
- Do not marry simply because you can.
- Marry because you have thought it all through.
- Marry because this person is someone who shares your values.
- Marry because the positives outweigh any negatives.
- Marry because you are prepared for what could happen if it does not work out as planned.
- Marry because you have your eyes wide open about every aspect of it.
- Marry because your love has depth and weight.
- Marry because you could not see yourself with another soul and the thought of not being legally united is anathema.

Wishing you luck and love!

AFTERWORD: HOW WILL YOUR LOVE LIVE ON?

JIM OBERGEFELL

If you have decided to say "I do," congratulations! I wish you and your future spouse every happiness as you begin the greatest and most meaningful adventure of your life. There's no telling what your future holds!

You might be wondering, *What comes next?* That is a question many of us ask ourselves every day. Marriage gives added dimensions to that question; marriage adds a sense of importance, meaning, and poignancy to our lives.

After more than twenty years together, my late husband, John Arthur, and I decided to marry. We wanted to say "I do" and make our commitment to each other public and legal. Thanks to the courage of Edie Windsor and the Supreme Court decision bearing her name, we could marry and have the federal government acknowledge our relationship. We knew what was coming next for us: John would soon take his last breath because he was dying of ALS, a progressive neurological disease. We said our vows and made our promises while we still could. All we wanted was to live out John's remaining days as husband and husband.

We never imagined where that short ceremony inside a medical jet in Maryland would lead. Shortly after we wed, friends introduced us to civil rights attorney Al Gerhardstein. Although the federal government recognized our marriage, Ohio, our home state, did not. We learned in difficult and painful ways the consequences of unequal treatment for same-sex couples. The opportunity to challenge this unequal treatment was a daunting decision, but it was nothing more than an extension of our decisions to become a couple, to build a life together, and to finally marry. It was simply the right thing to do. I also discovered that giving myself completely to one person made it easy to give of myself to others.

Ultimately, John and I decided to fight for each other, for our marriage, and for people across the nation. Our attorney filed a case in Ohio on our behalf; eventually, this case became one of the six cases that were consolidated for the U.S. Supreme Court with the name *Obergefell v. Hodges*. John and I had the opportunity to live up to our promises to love, honor, and protect each other, and to have those promises impact the world in a positive way.

Over the course of our legal fight, and especially since the Supreme Court ruling, I have been stopped innumerable times by people who want to shake my hand, thank me, share photos, and tell me stories about themselves or someone they love. I feel as if I am part of thousands of marriages across our country. That is a wonderful gift and an unexpectedly meaningful legacy for my husband.

Marriage is more than the sum of two people. When I said "I do" to John, I also said "I do" to the greater good, to people like us, and to people who believe in equality, fairness, and equal justice under the law. Our marriage became larger than the two of us. I hope you find that to be the case as you begin your married life together.

Say "I do" and make those promises to the love of your life. Embrace every day as if it's your last. Use your marriage to work for the greater good. Protect the next generation by working to end youth homelessness. Support HIV/AIDS organizations. Volunteer at your local school or for other organizations. No matter what it is, find a way to make your marriage matter not only to the two of you but also to others. Above all, be an example of love and commitment because that's how we change hearts and minds.

The old maxim "one person can change the world" is true. It is even more true and meaningful when you change the world with the love of your life. I was fortunate: the love and commitment that John and I had for each other helped to make our world a better place and we did it hand in hand with many other plaintiffs who fought beside me for their partners, spouses, and children. I found my purpose and my passion because I was lucky enough to find John first.

Our love for one another lives on in marriages across the nation—how will your love live on?

ACKNOWLEDGMENTS

First and foremost, my deepest gratitude to the many lesbian, gay, bisexual, transgender, and queer people who collectively got us to this moment when we have the privilege to consider whether marriage is right for our individual circumstances. To the drag queens at Stonewall who were sick of police abuse and inspired us all to rise up. To each victim of the AIDS pandemic, whose death was not in vain, for every loss was a cornerstone building a movement. To the countless activists, gay, straight, and otherwise, vocal and quiet, who demanded dignity and continue to do so in the face of ongoing bigotry and apathy.

To the plaintiffs in all the marriage cases that won the freedom to marry: you risked opening your hearts and homes to the public, proving our love is deserving of legitimacy under the law. I am grateful to the many clients who, for twenty years, have entrusted me to advise and sometimes strongly nudge; I acknowledge with deep regret all those for whom marriage came too late or was simply not enough.

All hail NCLR! For forty years, the National Center for Lesbian Rights has embodied undaunted perseverance and astounding brainpower. Props to Kate Kendell and Shannon Minter. Special thanks to Family Law Director Cathy Sakimura for the detailed read of this manuscript and spot-on suggested changes.

Among NCLR's brilliant ideas was to pull together a ragtag group of forty-five trailblazing LGBT family law practitioners from around the country some dozen years ago, known as the National Family

Law Advisory Council. We meet annually in San Francisco for two days of discussion, motivation, and brainstorming. Heartfelt appreciation to my NFLAC family—and I don't use "family" lightly, as you all have raised me—and to the broader community of lawyers in the Family Law Institute; your collective wisdom has been endlessly helpful in presenting this material.

I thank my SAGE family and especially our fearless leader, Michael Adams, for the support on this project. Services and Advocacy for GLBT Elders does amazing, effective, compassionate work, and I'm so very proud to serve as co-chair of our national board.

Immense appreciation to the fourteen splendid folks who contributed cameos; your decades of experience in the trenches helping LGBT individuals and couples came through in the wonderful submissions you shared. I'm eternally grateful you took the time out from your harried lives to contribute and to review the draft manuscript. It's also nice to share the horror of a writing deadline.

My greatest indebtedness is to my editor, Julie R. Enszer. You are the midwife who birthed this book. As a kid I dreamed of being a journalist—until I was first edited at the University of Pennsylvania newspaper. That's because I wasn't edited by someone as smart, kind, and utterly in tune as you are. Your idea for this book, which led you to find me (thank you, Professor Martha Ertman!) was born of your genuine goal to educate and inspire our community. I hope I've done your vision justice.

To Emily, Ben, Maredith, and the rest of the soulful sherpas at The New Press, thank you for your patience with this first-timer. I'm thrilled beyond measure to be a small part of the important social justice work that you publish.

To Steve Kozlowski: thank you for your careful lawyering and for being such a dear friend.

Huge hugs to Jerry Chasen: what a road we've trod together! Thank you for your early read and for your enduring friendship. It's a sheer joy to share passions with you.

Ivy league cheerleader claps for Kira Willig, family lawyer extraordinaire, for your deep read and excellent edits.

Shout-outs to supportive stalwarts without whom this book would have been an even greater slog, including Betsy Wise, David Boyer, Roxanne Naomi Schwartz, Abby Corbett, Michael Bath, Michael

Graubert, Crispy Soloperto, Leslie Cohen and Beth Suskin, LoAnn Halden, Brian Jacobson, Carmen and Ana Sofia Pelaez, Nadine Smith, and too many more to possibly mention (see how I benefit from an editor?). Laura Glass, you're a complete treasure. And thank you to the divine Paul Crockett for believing in me from before the start of my career.

Ibis Lynn Cejas is my office manager but really much more; my right and left hands, and, truth be told, my brain. She manages to hold down the fort while I pursue tremendous undertakings like this book and suing to overturn the Florida adoption and marriage bans. Ibis did the graphics for this book, and probably could have written it, too. Working with Ibis since the late 1990s is the greatest blessing of my career. Gracias, lady.

In the process of writing this book I lost my father, who taught me everything about everything. I'm grateful to my Forever Daddy for more than I could express but especially for the unconditional love. I only hope there are no grammatical errors in this book to sully his memory.

Todah rabah and much love to my mommy; you're my biggest champion, always my first editor, and you have taught me what it takes to make a marriage work (separate bathrooms and separate closets!).

And to save the best for last: Lydia Martin—my wife, love of my life, my inspiration, the actual writer in the family. We went through so much as this book was coming to fruition—such deep losses—and we've emerged stronger. Thank you so much for putting up with my utter craziness and for being the greatest blessing in my life. I like to think we'd have been as solid and content absent marriage. But it's nice not to have to wonder. *A tu lado, sea el bueno sea el malo. A tu lado, lo mejor que me ha pasado.*

APPENDIX: SELECTED RESOURCES

Governmental Organizations

Free Application for Federal Student Aid (FAFSA)
fafsa.ed.gov
800-4FED-AID

Internal Revenue Service
irs.gov

Medicaid
medicaid.gov
877-267-2323

Medicare
medicare.gov
800-MEDICARE

Office of Personnel Management
opm.gov
202-606-1800

Social Security Administration
ssa.gov
800-772-1213

United States Citizenship and Immigration Services
uscis.gov
800-375-5283

Advocacy Organizations Serving the LGBT Community

American Civil Liberties Union
aclu.org
212-549-2500

Equality Federation
equalityfederation.org
415-252-0510

Family Equality Council
familyequality.org
617-502-8700

Freedom for All Americans
freedomforallamericans.org
202-601-0187

Gay and Lesbian Alliance Against Defamation (GLAAD)
glaad.org
323-634-2043

GLBTQ Legal Advocates and Defenders (GLAD)
glad.org
617-426-1350

Gay, Lesbian, and Straight Education Network (GLSEN)
glsen.org
212-727-0135

Human Rights Campaign
hrc.org
800-777-4723

Immigration Equality
immigrationequality.org
212-714-2904

Lambda Legal
lambdalegal.org
212-809-8585

National Center for Lesbian Rights
nclrights.org
800-528-6257

National Center for Transgender Equality
transequality.org
202-642-4542

National LGBTQ Task Force
thetaskforce.org
202-393-5177

National LGBT Bar Association
lgbtbar.org
202-637-7661

Outserve/SLDN (Servicemembers Legal Defense Network)
www.outserve-sldn.org
800-538-7418

PFLAG
pflag.org
202-467-8180

Services and Advocacy for GLBT Elders (SAGE)
sageusa.org
212-741-2247

Servicemembers, Partners, Allies for Respect and Tolerance for All (SPART*A)
spartapride.org

Transgender Law Center
transgenderlawcenter.org
415-865-0176

Transgender Legal Defense and Education Fund
transgenderlegal.org
646-862-9396

Religious Organizations Serving the LGBT Community

Affirmation
affirmation.org

Association of Welcoming & Affirming
  Baptists
awab.org
240-242-9220

DignityUSA
dignityusa.org
800-877-8797

Keshet
keshetonline.org
617-524-9227

Metropolitan Community Churches
mccchurch.org
310-360-8640

More Light Presbyterians
mlp.org

Muslims for Progressive Values
mpvusa.org
323-696-2678

ReconcilingWorks: Lutherans for Full
  Participation
reconcilingworks.org
651-665-0861

Reconciling Pentecostals International
rpifellowship.com
219-871-1033

Room for All
roomforall.com
201-364-4538

Unitarian Universalist Association
uua.org
617-742-2100

Other Helpful Sites to Visit

American Academy of Adoption Attorneys
adoptionattorneys.org

American Academy of Assisted Repro-
  ductive Technology Attorneys
aaarta.org

DocuBank
docubank.com

Financial Literacy and Education
  Commission
mymoney.gov

Marriage Equality FAQ
marriageequalityfacts.org

National Association of Elder Law Attorneys (NAELA)
naela.org

INDEX

OTHER LGBTQ-RELATED TITLES
FROM THE NEW PRESS

Bordered Lives: Transgender Portraits from Mexico by Kike Arnal

Five Bells: Being LGBT in Australia by Jenny Papalexandris

Hold Tight Gently: Michael Callen, Essex Hemphill, and the Battlefield of AIDS by Martin Duberman

LGBTQ Stats: Lesbian, Gay, Bisexual, Transgender, and Queer People by the Numbers by David Deschamps and Bennett L. Singer (forthcoming)

Love Unites Us: Winning the Freedom to Marry in America by Kevin M. Cathcart and Leslie J. Gabel-Brett, editors

Lyudmila and Natasha: Russian Lives by Misha Friedman

The Martin Duberman Reader: The Essential Historical, Biographical, and Autobiographical Writings by Martin Duberman

Pride & Joy: Taking the Streets of New York City by Jurek Wajdowicz

Queer America: A People's GLBT History of the United States by Vicki L. Eaklor

A Saving Remnant: The Radical Lives of Barbara Deming and David McReynolds by Martin Duberman

Ties That Bind: Familial Homophobia and Its Consequences by Sarah Schulman

Waiting to Land: A (Mostly) Political Memoir, 1985–2008 by Martin Duberman

PUBLISHING IN THE PUBLIC INTEREST

Thank you for reading this book published by The New Press. The New Press is a nonprofit, public interest publisher. New Press books and authors play a crucial role in sparking conversations about the key political and social issues of our day.

We hope you enjoyed this book and that you will stay in touch with The New Press. Here are a few ways to stay up to date with our books, events, and the issues we cover:

- Sign up at www.thenewpress.com/subscribe to receive updates on New Press authors and issues and to be notified about local events
- Like us on Facebook: www.facebook.com/newpressbooks
- Follow us on Twitter: www.twitter.com/thenewpress

Please consider buying New Press books for yourself; for friends and family; or to donate to schools, libraries, community centers, prison libraries, and other organizations involved with the issues our authors write about.

The New Press is a 501(c)(3) nonprofit organization. You can also support our work with a tax-deductible gift by visiting www.thenewpress.com/donate.